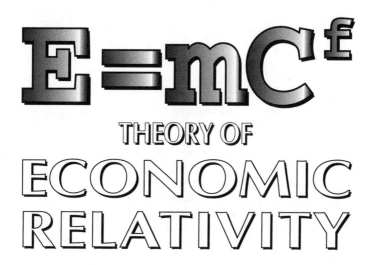

$E=mC^f$

THEORY OF
ECONOMIC
RELATIVITY

THE SOLUTION FOR THE 21ST CENTURY

CAPITALISM TO THE NEXT LEVEL

MARK PASH, CFP

$$E = m\,C^{\,f}$$

For information contact:
Global Community Press
P. O. Box 260874
Encino, CA 91426-0874
(800) 281-9054

Editor: Jack Barnard
Cover & Book Design: Dotti Albertine

Library of Congress
Catalog Card Number: 99-60135

ISBN: 0-9669653-0-2

First Edition

C O N T E N T S

Acknowledgements   vii
Introduction   viii
E=mCf   xvi

SECTION I
DESCRIPTIVE

1 Fiscal Power   1
2 Monetary Power   3
3 Link Between Monetary And Fiscal Policy   13
4 Federal Economic Policies   17

SECTION II
WHAT'S WRONG?

5 Problems with Monetary Systems   24
6 Flaws of Capitalism   32
7 Problems and Limitations of One System   39
8 Statistics and formulas   48
9 Inflation vs. Growth   55

SECTION III
HOW TO IMPROVE

10 Why Diversify the Monetary Delivery Systems?   62
11 Additional Monetary Expansion   69
12 Elimination of Excess Inflation   75
13 Debt and Equity   79
14 Implementation   82
15 Current & Potential New Monetary Delivery Systems   87
16 Restructure the Economics of Federal Governments   101
17 Educate the Public   106

CONCLUSION

Vision/ Other Theories/ Paradoxes/ Summary   111

GLOSSARY

An Explanation of Terms   123

$$E = mC^{£}$$

A healthy and thriving <u>E</u>conomy depends

on a diversified and expansive <u>M</u>onetary system,

free private <u>C</u>apital enterprise

and an efficient, recirculating <u>F</u>iscal system

ACKNOWLEDGMENTS

First, I wish to thank Joel Gray, CFP, for motivating me to start and to finish the difficult task of explaining new concepts outside the norm.

Second, I would like to thank all the writers, authors, researchers and economists — as well as Economist Magazine — for their contributions to the development of this philosophy. I was inspired by the work of many, but did not specifically pinpoint credit in outlining this new concept.

Third, I owe much to the writing talents of Jack Barnard. His down-to-earth style has brought the concepts contained in this book directly to the people — at all levels of our global society.

Lastly, I want to thank my wife, Ruth, my family, and all my friends, clients and employees who have had to put up with my "out of the box" ideas.

A special thank you to my partner Gary Benson, CFP, who allowed me time away from my practice...and to Sunny Nabate for helping administratively.

The thought process behind this book started for me with my university studies. I was a business major experienced in practical applications. All my economics classes — and the prevailing economic paradigms — were focused on the strict theories of the day. This perplexed me then, it still does now. This puzzlement continued into the inflationary experience of the late '70s, and the domino-like collapse of many of the international monetary systems around the globe. I've known for years that monetary policy should be an integral element in the world. I just haven't been able to figure out why the economists of academia have so failed to adequately improve the system. In fact, I had been waiting for them to come out with a solution.

Finally, a few years ago, I entered a congressional race to take the debate to the people. To my chagrin, I found that 99% of our electorate in my well educated and affluent district didn't have the slightest idea what I was talking about. I suppose that this book is a result of this lack of knowledge.

As you begin the journey of reading $E=mCf$, I want you to know right from the start that it is purposely written in a simple language so that everyone can understand and grasp its concepts — **not just economists!** Although I encourage economists to read this book in its entirety, it is certainly not just for them. After all, we can't expect "them" — the politicians, economists, philosophers, and so forth — to do all our thinking and planning for us. Thomas Jefferson said it very well almost two hundred years ago: **"Freedom and ignorance cannot coexist."**

$E=mC\!f$ is a book written for all people interested in improving our culture, our country, and our world — *anyone who has concern about our future!* I have limited economic jargon, mathematical formulas and the like and I've tried to apply common sense for describing and improving our current structure.

Economists and others who care about the global predicament need to have open minds. I'll tell you right now: if you're a socialist, you won't like this concept of capitalism. If you're a laissez-faire — pure market classical economist — if you think the market solves everything, you won't like it either. I simply ask you to try to open your understanding to the next level of our economic world.

In other words, I want to make my doctrine understandable to many so that we can implement quality change. I want to encourage all economists to begin and continue the debate on vastly improving the monetary system.

Having said that, let me state this loud and clear: *the economic systems of the world are in need of change!* The current debate regarding 19th and 20th Century economics provides no viable vision for the 21st Century. Over the years, I've listened to a rainbow of politicians and economists and I've read the mountains of literature being presented by both sides. About the only consensus thus far is the absence of a real solution to improve our macroeconomic systems.

There are three major powers of a sovereign nation: (1) military-foreign policy, (2) tax and spend (fiscal policy), (3) money creation (monetary policy). We read about the military on a daily basis, the budget and taxation are always in the news, but have you noticed the lack of discussion on the last power?

Let's say it like it is: there is virtually *no* discussion on our monetary power.

This dismays me, because I believe monetary improvement is the key to the economic future of our nation and the world. I've been working on this issue for many years. **The purpose of this book that I call $E=mCf$, is to christen the debate to vastly improve our monetary system, and consequently create an economic vision for the 21st Century.**

I want to encourage the governments of the world to establish commissions or otherwise instigate meaningful dialogue to review the monetary systems. For over 80 years now, we have had a single solitary system delivering one of the paramount functions of a government, the power to create money. This simply does not make sense!

The antiquated banking institutions (dating back to the last century) and the current commercial banking structure cannot hope to meet the needs of 21st century capitalism. This inadequacy greatly contributes to an unbalanced budget, less-than-optimum expansion of the economies and global currency crises.

But having said this, **it just does not make financial (or common) sense to correct the fiscal — tax and spend — side of government without reforming the monetary side.**

Look at recent history. Where there has been private and governmental investment (both fiscal and monetary), we have had long term economic success. Before government took such an active role, the barons of the industrial revolution were responsible for spurts of growth and capital infusion. This capital led the way to opportunity and growth.

But private capital is very fickle and narrow-casted, so this arrangement resulted in cycles of panic — deep recession and depression — *until* the government was established as a partner in growth. **My goal is to empower the government to be a more efficient partner** so we can accomplish the necessary programs to insure our future.

A word about capitalism. Capitalism is grand. Capitalism is the only real economic system that has emerged in the world. (Capitalism is truly a system because it embraces the whole of society and operates on its own terms.) It does not really need government or any other traditional institutional framework to make it operate. But capitalism is far from perfect. Unfortunately, there are several flaws in a pure free market system. $E=mCf$ compensates for those flaws and provides the remedy.

GOAL OF THIS BOOK

$E=mCf$ will reveal the glaring inadequacies of the current system; explore the reasons to have a diversified, non-inflationary and expansive monetary supply; present ways to avoid excessive inflation; show how some fiscal policy matters can be better solved by monetary policy; and finally, examine a different government structure and accountability system.

The solutions offered will present methods for resolving balanced budget dilemmas, for stretching the growth cycle (less frequent and severe recessions), for lowering unemployment and creating *higher quality* jobs and for solving the economic problems of the inner city and other poorer areas. Currently, we see severe financial crisis pop up daily in various international economical systems. But we have seen them before — both in the U.S. and the rest of the world — and we will continue to see them until we attain the next level of capitalism.

More and more we are part of a global village, symbiotically connected, dependent on each other in ever-increasing ways. $E=mCf$ will also provide the economic avenues to accomplish programs for the betterment of not just our country but the world.

My wish is that this book reshapes your concept of a federal government's economic responsibility and gives you a host of strategic restructuring ideas for future global economic development.

THE STATUS QUO

Largely because economic experts like to cloak their pronouncements in obscure, pseudo-scientific jargon, the popular culture does not understand economic and monetary machinery. Therefore people must put their trust in these experts, who presumably have the best interests of the general public at heart. The sentiment is glorious, but these experts are self-interested mortals. Can they truly operate in trust on behalf of the people they service?

The answer is no!, even if they try. They're not perfect. Therefore, the monetary power must reenter the debate, bringing with it the knowledge of the past and a keen eye on the future. Most importantly, implementation of monetary power cannot be limited to only a few delivery systems. Similar to the structure of our fiscal power, monetary power needs many delivery systems.

As you read my book, I want you to ask yourselves the following questions:

1. Why have *monetary systems failed* so frequently around the world?

2. Why is there only *one major system* to *create and infuse new money* into our economy?

3. Why is *new money created* only *through debt*?

4. Why do *central banks raise interest rates* to control inflation, at the same time directly *killing growth, creating unemployment* and hardship?

5. Why do *government policies* have to be mainly *implemented by fiscal* (tax and spend) *policy*?

6. Why does our *current monetary system over lend* that *cause boom-and-bust* scenarios?

7. Why is over *15% of the Federal budget* (interest on debt) *not controlled by Congress*?

WHAT YOU ARE ABOUT TO READ

The seventeen chapters of $E=mC\!f$ are divided into three sections.

The first section **(DESCRIPTIVE)** contains four chapters and lays the foundation for the rest of the book. It explains fiscal power, monetary power, the link between monetary and fiscal policy, and federal economic policies. If you're a trained economist, treat this first section as a review of what you know. If you're a lay person, new to macroeconomics, these chapters are essential for grasping the ins and outs of the status quo.

The second section **(WHAT'S WRONG?)** uses five chapters to present the problems with our current way of managing the economy. Before going on to innovative solutions, first we must create an agreement as to what's wrong with the way we're doing it. As my mom used to say, "you don't fix something that's not broken," so this section shows mom and the rest of you readers what's broken or near breakdown in our current way of doing things. In this section, we dive into the problems with monetary systems, the flaws of capitalism, the limitations of a one system structure, the shortcomings of statistics and formulas, and the symbiotic relationship between inflation and growth.

The last section **(HOW TO IMPROVE)** outlines the solutions and improvements for the problems presented in section two. This section has eight chapters which concern themselves with the reasons why monetary delivery systems should be diversified, innovations for additional monetary expansion, ways to eliminate excess inflation, the relationship between debt and equity, how to implement the ideas in this book, possibilities for new monetary delivery systems, bold steps to restructure the economics of federal governments, and reasons to educate the public regarding these innovations. The concluding chapter outlines my vision for the country and world if these changes are brought to reality, the error of other theories, and a review of the paradoxes and contradictions inherent in the complicated world of economics.

~~~~

We stand at the gateway to destiny. In just a few generations, we have negotiated great advances culturally, in business, medicine, technology and the like. All of this progress is dependent on a prosperous social environment, but, like an immovable gatekeeper, economics is holding these great advances back. Macroeconomics has been sadly lagging behind. This is the next area for a breakthrough.

E=mCf is my way of bringing economics into the 21st Century.

$$E = mC^f$$

The following is the proper macroeconomic structure for any and all countries who want to enjoy freedom-oriented capitalism.

E = A healthy and thriving **ECONOMY** is defined as one which emphasizes care for all humans, has an abundance of quality paying jobs, in turn creating sufficient consumers, resulting in a well-satisfied and educated populace.

m = A high quality, expansive **MONETARY** system concentrated on increasing a variety of goods and services and developing natural resources. Such a policy uses a diversified, efficient monetary system without excessive inflation. In other words, both debt and equity are utilized to infuse new money with private capital (old money) into private enterprise. Thus, more commerce is created, resulting in more tax revenues, supporting a democratic fiscal system.

C = A free private **CAPITAL** and enterprise system which promotes the Four I's: initiative, incentive, innovation, and investment. This factor is more important than monetary and fiscal policy but cannot exist for long without them.

f = a diversified **FISCAL** system centered around a balanced budget, with economic checks and balances. The recirculation of wealth (demand stimulation) and long range public investments (infrastructure, education, legal structure) must work hand-in-hand with sensible regulations to overcome the flaws of pure open market (Laissez Faire) capitalism. The fiscal system funds a series of laws and enforcement which is absolutely essential to the eventual success of any capitalistic system.

Of course, this Fiscal side cannot be confiscatory. By this, I mean we can't take too much in taxes to stifle growth and incentive. Nor should we take too little so that we don't have an effective recirculation of wealth for those who do not participate efficiently. This book does not discuss this balance, but in the mid-to-late 90's, income taxes seem to fall within reasonable percentage parameters. Just remember this, with diverse monetary turnover (velocity of circulation) comes an increase in total taxes, which enables lower tax rates.

The current U.S. fiscal (f) and private capital (C) systems are developed and progressing. It's our monetary delivery systems that need complete restructuring. This does not mean an elimination of central banking systems. **It only means increasing their methods of disbursement.** Once that is accomplished we can create a domestic industrial complex effectively funded by fiscal (tax revenues), monetary (new money) and private capital (old money).

Then, and only then, will we take human existence to the next level.

Please note, with the number of variables currently involved, reducing human commercial behavior to a mathematical formula is all-but impossible. **So, $E=mCf$ is not meant to be a mathematical formula.** In actual fact, it disputes the notion that human-commercial behavior can be reduced to formulas and should be completely guided by statistics. Still, the structure, $E=mCf$, allows for the only synergetic relationship between the private sector and the two economic powers of a central government.

$E=mCf$ is the guide used in macroeconomic development. It is a beginning general descriptive principle to which we can develop our future and guide governmental decisions.

Nonetheless, there is one exception! The only one! The measurement of *inflation*. Monetary authorities need to have several ways of measuring inflation, not with one number but with a range of inflationary measurements. With the advent of computers and our current research facilities, this should not be a difficult task and should be easier to control with diversified delivery systems. Also, as we evolve to a global economy, these figures need to be examined within a more global perspective.

With $E=mCf$ you mainly have to measure the inflation range and eliminate excess inflation. Monetary authorities have several inflationary formulas to guide them and once a diversified delivery system is agreed on...**we should just let the people (commerce) go to it!** Bottom line: this is the soul of $E=mCf$. **It allows the free enterprise system to expand and reach new heights for the 21st century without collapsing because of its flaws.** More importantly, benefits are brought to all — workers and owners.

It is truly amazing to me that this myriad of workers, firms and households — acting without visible coordination and guided mainly by self-interest — manage to produce such extraordinary benefits. The "Free" market with all its faults is still a marvel.

The ultimate test for any science is the ability of its rules and theories to predict outcomes, and by that standard, economics is a vastly underdeveloped discipline. When their models and predictions fail, economists say that political impulses or human psychology has disrupted the equations.

Within the entire macroeconomic-monetary structure, economists attempt to measure and control money supply by controlling interest rates, reserves and open market operation. They make their decisions based on the kinds of formulas that are used in the scientific world, such as mathematics and physics. They especially try to mimic physics, particularly in trying to control monetary policy, but 20th Century physicists have moved beyond the clockwork laws of Newton to the relativity of Einstein, a vastly improved conception of reality. Economists seem unable to follow them on a macroeconomic level. $E=mCf$ is their guide to the future.

Unfortunately, no matter how sophisticated the formulas, our limited system of new money distribution is so narrow and biased it cannot efficiently introduce new capital (money) without serious miscalculations. If these formulas work for anything, it's to create economic upheavals and chaos — which they certainly do from time-to-time.

My hope is that this book nudges these economists to the next podium of development where we rely less on old banking systems and the array of statistics and formulas used to measure and control an inept system. In truth, these mathematical calculations are less important because they cannot be implemented by an imperfect system run by imperfect human beings.

With a properly diversified monetary system and an efficient fiscal system, the flaws of capitalism will be overcome. Then, and only then, can we let private enterprise run with the ball and create an economic well being a cut above the current U.S. economy. In the United States at present time, we have progressed. If you compare us to the historical well being of past populations, we're far better off. All that's left is to restructure capitalism in the manner outlined in this book. Then we can fly into the new millennium!

DESCRIPTIVE

<u>1</u> FISCAL POWER

*F*iscal power describes the governmental authority to *tax* and *spend*. In this country, fiscal policy delineates the basic power of Congress to set taxing and spending amounts. There is often considerable controversy about the appropriate parameters of fiscal policy and the balance between what the government should spend and what it should tax.

This is not a book to discuss the fiscal policies of a federal government. Still, it is absolutely essential that the powers of the government be strong and well-defined in these areas to compensate for the major flaws of free market capitalism. (See Chapter 6)

Over the last two hundred years, we've had every conceivable combination of Federal tax and spend policies. We have had high, middle and low taxation, we've had high, moderate and low spending. Personally, I think it's time to bite the bullet here, we just can't seem to get it right. **Minor or major adjustments in the amount we spend and tax will not solve the problem nor will it create an adequate future.** Our attention is misguided. A tax cut here and there will not stimulate an abundant, 21st Century economy, nor will a little more fiscal spending. Economic history has more than proven this point!

Of course, no government taxing system can be confiscatory. Confiscatory taxes result in economic collapse. In other words, a tax rate of 99% is too high and 1% is far too low to overcome the failings of capitalism. (See Chapter 6)

In the 19th Century, we had no income tax and nominal government spending. In the early 20th Century, we had a very low flat income tax (which stimulated nothing during the Great Depression). In the latter half of this century, we have experienced excessive governmental spending with relatively high taxes. Regardless, I much prefer the economic condition of the *average* American during the latter half of the 20th Century to life in the previous 150 years. Now it's time to step into an advanced phase of capitalism. This book outlines that next step.

The governmental fiscal policy consists of three principal parts: 1) the purchase of goods and services; 2) taxation; and 3) transfer of payments (i.e., unemployment and Medicare). Partly because of the huge volume of its economic operations, inevitably, the government's fiscal policies directly affect the functioning of the economy. Nearly seventy years ago, the revolutionary economist John Maynard Keynes introduced the idea that a national government can greatly help the economy of the country, especially regarding war and recession. Keynes advocated an active government fiscal policy of deficit spending on public works and other projects and the maintenance during depressions of an unbalanced budget to increase the **aggregate demand** for goods and services.

Unfortunately, Keynes only recommended fiscal policy as a counteractive measure. He should have more adequately explored monetary policy as an additional way to progress the economy and guide us out of war and recession; and create a 21st century capitalistic economic structure.

2 MONETARY POWER

When you read about the economic functions of governments, 90% of what makes the headlines focuses on **fiscal policy**, meaning, *the rate at which they should tax* and, consequently, *how much they should spend*. But there is another major economic governmental power, which is the creation of new money and its infusion into the country (or world). This is called **monetary policy**. Since 1932, the majority of economic congressional debate was centered on fiscal policy, while last century, most of the debate was centered on monetary policy.

In my opinion, monetary policy is *at least* as important as fiscal policy.

The following is a very brief discussion of how new money is created and infused into the economy. Since I am American, most of the terms and processes will be reflective of U.S. monetary systems, but the breadth of this book also includes ways to improve all monetary — **new money** — systems in the world.

If you need a more complete understanding of money, monetary policy, and its history, there are many books available on this subject in university libraries and book stores. These books are mostly historical and explanatory; their solutions are limited to improving the current single system and its operations and regulations. $E=mCf$ offers the entire solution.

OLD MONEY

Historically, almost all capital investment utilizes "old money." Every financial institution is basically an intermediary — the middleman between lenders (investors) and borrowers (receivers). Therefore, the essence of finance is an exchange across time — transactions between the past and the future. Old money, the surplus accumulated from past endeavors, is made available to new ventures with the promise of future rewards for both.

From the largest investment banks and Wall Street brokerages to the smallest credit union or neighborhood savings and loan, the major, overriding function is to collect money from people and businesses who have accumulated a surplus and deliver it to the debtors who need to use it.

The surplus accumulated from previous ventures is made available to new and old commerce with the promise of future rewards for both. **This is the definition of "Old Money"**. If a bank borrows money from one group, the depositors, and then lends it to someone else, the borrowers, this is a straight forward function as an intermediary. No new money is created.

For all its seeming contradictions and complexities, Wall Street is as simple as this. **Do not confuse old money with new money!**

NEW MONEY

In this book, I am not concerned with the operations of "Old Money", but I am seriously concerned with the distribution of "New Money". When you examine financial instruments, you should be aware of whether they're new or old money. Most is old money. **The major source of new money is the commercial banking system, controlled by some form of**

central banking oversight and control. In the United States, the controller is the Federal Reserve Board. In England it's the Bank of England, in Japan, the Bank of Japan, in Germany it's the Bundstbank, which, by the way, is evolving into the new central banking system of the Maastricht Treaty, starting with eleven countries.

Down through the ages, this ability to create new money has been the power of sovereigns. In present day, money creation has been delegated to the technocrats of the central bank, who inherited this power from private banks who inherited it from kings and before them, the temple priests of ancient civilization, endowed by God with the authority to consecrate, enFiat, the currency of their society.

Unfortunately, this process — almost magical in its simplicity — remains a mystery and hidden to most modern day citizens. Money owes its existence to the special domain of politics. Money is the bailiwick of the state. And, like all things political, the vagaries of money are controlled by imperfect human beings, influenced by conflicting pressures and prone to error. Money is the web in a cultural infrastructure that gives a prize or penalizes, that encourages or impedes. Money can either raise high the banner of democracy or stand like a great boulder in its path. **21st century democratic capitalism does not have to have winners and losers — we can all be winners — it's just that some will win more!**

One of the lesser objectives of this book is to simply unlock the mystery of new money and make more citizens aware of monetary power. **After all, how can you improve a system without its citizens (and lead-**

ers) having enough understanding to create an adequate debate?

THE COMMERCIAL BANKING SYSTEM

In the U.S., there are basically two main types of
monetary institutions — or issuers of new money:
the Federal Reserve and their regulated commercial
banks, such as Bank of America, Citibank, Wells
Fargo and Chase. **These banks are by far the largest
issuers of new money.** They do it by new lending, by
expanding their outstanding loans. Central banks and
treasury departments around the world do have monetary creation powers, but these powers are not used
nearly to the extent of the commercial banks. The
Federal Reserve and Treasury have many available
ways to regulate these institutions but basically there
is only one main system for its delivery.
Unfortunately, with only one powerful system and
only one type of new money delivery, errors can and
have created erroneous upheavals in economies all
over the world.

Here's a very simple explanation of how new money
is created by these commercial banks. Let's say you
make a $1000 bank deposit. Because of regulatory
privilege with the Federal Reserve, the bank can loan
out a multiple of this figure, let's say $7000. **The size
of this multiple, which is called the reserve requirement, is regulated by the Federal Reserve. This
$6000 difference, new money, is placed in demand
deposits — the checking accounts of its borrowers.**
Therefore, the bulk of the new money is not created
by printing, it is a simple entry in the personal and
business checking accounts of borrowers.

Most of what we call spending money exists as cash,

checking account deposits and other new types of accounts (ATM-credit cards). If the public for some reason wants to hold more money in hard cash, the Bureau of Engraving prints more bills and the Federal Reserve distributes the currency through the banking systems, *but the printing itself does not create new money* — since cash is simply substituted for existing checking account deposits.

The major creation of money is really based on bank-created debt. The average citizen is unaware of this concept and this is why there are many critics of the money system. They insist that money should be real and based on something tangible from the past, accumulated wealth like gold, not a banker's estimate of the future. Personally, I don't know why either limitation should be the sole basis for monetary creation.

For the most part, banks — large and small — have been the most secure business enterprises in America, sheltered by government from failure like no other sector. Their deposits are protected by the FDIC (Federal Deposit Insurance Corp.) and if a bank has problems, the Federal Reserve will lend it capital to increase its reserves. Finally, if a bank fails, it's just merged into others.

Since 1913, the Federal Reserve's efforts have been relatively successful in protecting our banking institutions. Of course, there has been one exception, the crash of 1929 and the subsequent panic that closed nearly half the banks in America. (Some exception!)

Every banker works to take maximum advantage of their monetary-lending powers, to be "booked up", reserves fully committed to loaning the last available dollar at the very highest interest income. This means that if they have $1000 in deposits, they are allowed to loan out $7000. They make every attempt to loan this $7000 whether the borrowers need it or not! In slack times, if a bank can't find enough borrowers to soak up its credit capacity, then it buys government bonds that pay interest using the same money-creating process. This process links it to the fiscal system where ultimately, the interest is paid on the debt. (See Chapter 3)

This sounds simple enough, but not all is so idyllic. Banks have had dangerous histories. They are run by humans, who, left to their own impulses, can be tempted to expand their loans and create new money infinitely — collecting more and more interest income, their main source of profit. Eventually the system forces over-monetary expansion and if not stopped, collapses of its own greed in a frenzy of hyper-inflation. If it is stopped too drastically and quickly, it pulls the tablecloth from under the economy and causes an extreme and painful recession or depression.

The banks are restrained from doing this by the Federal Reserve and the central banks of the world. Unfortunately, their track record in this area is anything but spotless. (See Chapter 5 for the many examples of these failures.)

FEDERAL RESERVE (The Central Bank of the U.S.)

How does the current system work? The simple explanation is trust. People trust the banks and the system that controls them (Federal Reserve). People trust that banks will use this creation process prudently and make sound loans that will be repaid and they trust that the banks will keep enough cash on hand so that any depositor can get his money when he needs it. But if enough loans go bad and enough depositors became distrustful, they all go to the bank to withdraw their money at once. This was called a "run on the bank".

These runs were much more prevalent in the 19th century, and they usually ended in bank failures and padlocked doors. The Federal Reserve (Central Bank) was created in 1913 to protect the banking system from periodic liquidity crises — temporary shortages of money that lead to breakdown.

THE FED AS A DIRECT MONEY CREATOR

The Fed protects banks and the banking system through the discount windows at each of the twelve Federal Reserve Banks, providing short term loans to banks. Here, commercial banks routinely borrow hundreds of millions, even billions, every day to make up for temporary shortages in *their reserve requirements* (as set by the central bank, the amount of assets — cash, deposits needed — to be allowed to lend). **At the same time, increasing bank reserves is another way the central bank creates new money through the commercial banks.**

The other more important mechanism for the Fed is the *Open Market Desk* at its New York Federal Reserve Bank in the middle of Wall Street. This is where the Fed **buys with new money** and sells government securities (bills, notes and bonds) in the open market, in daily transactions running from five hundred million to billions. (See in Chapter 3 how

$E=mC^f$

the monetary power is pushed by fiscal policy.)

In both of the above options, the Fed creates new money with a key stroke of the computer terminal. When the Federal Reserve lends Treasury bonds to banks through the discount window, it simply credits the bank's account (money creation). It doesn't matter which bank got this "new money'. Once it's created, it increases the overall money supply and is free to float from one account to another through the entire banking system. In reverse, when a commercial bank repays its discount loan, money is extinguished by the Fed. By a simple entry in the ledger, money is withdrawn from circulation in the private economy.

If the Fed is too expansive in their open market operations, the circular game that results is what critics refer to as "printing press money." Economists call this *"monetarizing" the debt*. The central bank inflates the currency, the Treasury is off the hook. **This means the national debt is reduced**. Here's how it works: The Executive Branch (Treasury Dept.) borrows money from the private sector by selling new Treasury notes and bonds. In turn, the Fed buys up old T notes and bonds from the private sector or new ones from the Treasury with new money, which dilutes the resultant value of this debt. The end result? The Fed has more and more of the government's debt paper in its own portfolio — and the private economy winds up with an increased money supply.

THE FED AS A REGULATOR

In simplest terms, the Federal Reserve Board / Central banking system is the governor that sits alongside our economic system. The Fed's policies can stimulate the flow of lending, choke it off, or nudge it in a myriad of directions. Primarily, the Fed accomplishes this by either injecting more money into the system or withdrawing it; in other words, by creating or destroying money.

The Fed controls the issuance of new money by controlling the reserves requirement of commercial banks and the price of money (interest rates).

Of course, this is a very simplistic view of the Fed and its functions, but it is not the purpose of this book to be a text for description of central banking accounting, systems and operations.

Most books discuss the history and errors of monetary systems. Then, any recommendations to improve the current system is narrowed to just two things: the operational decision-making of central banks and who controls them, and the improvement of the current delivery system, which is commercial banking. **THIS IS NOT THE ANSWER!** In fact, this specific debate has hidden the real solution to the improvement of the world's monetary system.

The purpose of this book is to establish a new basic structure for a change in monetary systems and to start the debate for improvement. Human beings are resistant to change, but there is certainly nothing handed down by divine providence saying that this monetary power cannot be improved.

In short, $E=mCf$ is an attempt to inform the common man of the use of monetary power as a way to effect the kind of change that can be implemented from the bottom up. The reason is simple: most research on monetary systems ignores the development of many delivery systems, primarily focusing on how to more perfectly run the single current system. Unfortunately, humans and their institutions cannot be perfect, so this is an impossible task. Systems have to be established with this understanding. *The current world monetary system is not and will not ever be perfect!*

I will say this many times during the course of the book: **Diversity reduces the consequences of human errors.**

Virtually the entire macroeconomic fraternity attempts to measure and control money supply by using various and complex methods of controlling interest rates, reserves and open market operations (see page 10 and Glossary). They try their best to be good scientists, applying arcane, complicated mathematic/physics formulas to these systems.

Unfortunately, no matter how mysteriously or how efficiently these formulas are operated, our limited system of new money distribution is too **narrow and biased**. The inadequate system we suffer under today cannot possibly be the correct structure for 21st Century capitalism. I predict that one hundred years from now, we will look back on our current system and it will not even be close to the operating discipline of the time.

In fact, may I be so bold to say, as we approach the next millennium, the improvement of this system is the key to the future of the economic-capitalistic world!

DESCRIPTIVE

3 LINK BETWEEN MONETARY AND FISCAL POLICY

There are five major areas where fiscal policy and monetary policy are strategically linked with the economy. Fiscal policy is more directly linked to monetary policy than vice versa.

THE FIRST LINK
FISCAL PRESSURES FORCE MORE DEFICIT

In the current political nature of our world governments, constituents demand protection, services and support. When the revenue of a government is less than its expenditures (annual deficit), it borrows money to cover the deficit. This debt is then added to the national debt. The interest on this debt is part of the fiscal budget.

Instead of a monetary system funding part of our needs, our fiscal system picks up the slack and creates this debt. As of this writing, the national debt of our nation is 7 trillion dollars! **7 trillion dollars!**

THE SECOND LINK
NATIONAL DEBT FORCES MONETARY CREATION

The national debt is paid off in two ways — tax surpluses and money creation. Over the decades, tax surpluses have only nominally been used to repay any part of the national debt.

When the government is allowed to create new money, this is called monetarization of the debt. It has been used substantially more to reduce the debt than surpluses. The central bank — through its open market operations — creates new money with a tap tap tap of the computer terminal. Naturally, excessive monetarization breeds excessive inflation.

THE THIRD LINK
PROFITS OF MONETARY OPERATIONS
REDUCE FISCAL PRESSURE

In the creation of new money and the trading of government bonds, this monopolistic operation of the Central banks creates substantial profits. These profits are sent to the fiscal side of government as revenue just like income tax. Maybe, it should be sent somewhere else. (See Chapter 16)

THE FOURTH LINK
INTEREST ON DEBT
INCREASES FISCAL PRESSURE

Interest is charged on our national debt, which is paid by our taxes and is part of the annual budgeted expense of government. This is not a piddling item. In the U.S., this interest expense has approached 20% of the annual budget.

This variable interest expense, which is set by the Treasury on government bonds, depends on the rise and fall of interest rates. These interest rates are controlled by both the central banks (Federal Reserve) and the international capital markets. Obviously, if interest rates are rising, the cost of the national debt goes up — if interest rates decrease, this expense goes down. Therefore, a substantial part of the budget is not controlled by Congress, as it should be, and future Congresses are saddled with past debts.

Rising interest rates can hurt the economy and cause various social programs, such as unemployment compensation, to kick in, thereby raising government expenditures. Moreover, the lessened economic activity causes a decrease in tax revenues.

These increased social expenditures, combined with a decrease in revenues and the greater interest expense from carrying the national debt, causes budgetary deficits. Thus, additional pressure is put on the current monetary powers to once again tighten the money supply — usually by raising interest rates. These factors widen the budget deficit in a never-ending cycle of economic structure.

In plain talk, if interest rates go up, the deficit goes up. How in the world does this make sense? Talk about a Catch 22!

THE FIFTH LINK
COMMERCIAL BANKING

When the economy needs more new money creation, instead of lending, commercial banks buy government bonds. These bonds provide no risk at a reasonable rate of return. The government demand for money through its bonds also attracts old money into government bonds, thereby reducing availability to the private sector.

꽁꽁꽁꽁

Many economists feel that a reasonable amount of national debt as related to GNP is acceptable. Under the current structure of a federal government, I would agree. But this is the wrong structure. (See Chapter 16 for a more appropriate structure for 21st century capitalism.)

4 FEDERAL ECONOMIC POLICIES

The two major economic powers of a sovereign nation, fiscal (tax and spend) and monetary (new money), can both be implemented within two basic policies: expansive (liberal) or restrictive (conservative). The link between the two causes reactions in both. The following examines the four combinations that best describe federal economic policies.

CONSERVATIVE FISCAL CONSERVATIVE MONETARY

The first doctrine combines a *limited fiscal* policy with a *conservative monetary* policy. This configuration eventually leads to depression, recession and unemployment — not at all one's definition of a healthy economy.

Under a conservative fiscal system, government spending is very limited, resulting in *inadequate* aggregate demand. (See Chapter 6) In a conservative monetary system, the central bankers have raised interest rates, restricted loans or not allowed enough dispersal of new money. These banking practices, narrow and imperfect in both nature and scope, create an unwillingness on the part of companies and individuals to take out new loans because of the fear of continued economic downturn.

Unfortunately, global monetary policies and their

consequent systems have not evolved enough to fight depression or excess inflation without causing a recession.

The restrictive (limited) fiscal policy was followed by the U.S. Government from 1865-1932. When a conservative monetary policy compounded an economic downturn — without fiscal remedies — we entered the Great Depression. Then, when the monetary system attempted to lower interest and become expansive, this inadequate central banking system wasn't enough to pull the economy out of a depression. (In a downturn no one wants to expand their business. The rates may be low, but people are understandably too afraid to borrow.)

Modern day Japan provides a more recent example. In the midst of an unprecedented boom period, banks and financial institutions greatly over lent. Eventually the monetary system attempted to convert to a more conservative policy and to stop speculation by raising interest rates, but they were too late. A decade later, they're still trying to recover from the devastating recession that came out of their inadequate practices, and their financial structures are still quite problematical.

EXPANSIVE FISCAL (with deficit)
EXPANSIVE MONETARY

Another doctrine combines an *expansive fiscal* policy with an *expansive monetary* policy, *usually with deficit spending*. A fiscal policy of deficit government spending, along with an expansive monetary policy, can result in only one economic condition: hyper-inflation.

A number of Latin American nations provide prime examples for this scenario. Knowing that these liberal policies only lead to ruin, one must ask why these countries can't stop their excessive inflationary economies. The fact is, they have tried many fiscal solutions, none 100% successful.

What they need is an uncorrupted, diversified new money delivery system that uses equity as well as debt and has greater access to more people. This book will discuss these solutions.

EXPANSIVE FISCAL (with deficit)
CONSERVATIVE MONETARY

The next policy doctrine should be familiar to Americans. It is the one that the U.S. and many other nations have today: an *expansive fiscal* system — *usually with deficit spending* — with a *restrictive* (conservative), anti-inflationary (central banking) *monetary* policy.

In response to constituents' desires and wants, many governments have combined a liberal fiscal philosophy, usually with deficit spending, which forces monetary expansion. (See Chapter 3) This policy can easily cause excessive inflationary pressure. Spending that doesn't produce goods and services — except for the necessary borrowing to pay for the deficit — has resulted in our galloping national debt. Since the interest on this debt is charged to the fiscal side, this borrowing increases the annual deficit even more.

One way this National debt gets paid off is by having a fiscal surplus. This has happened very rarely over the last two hundred years and has been so small that it could never comes close to paying off any sizable debt. The other way to handle the debt would be to monetarize it, meaning to create new money to pay it off. Of course, this is also limited because of the ignition of excess inflation. Again, no production of goods and service.

Therefore, this policy forces the monetary system to adopt the single goal of fighting inflation and limiting economic growth. An Expansive-Restrictive system plods along with inadequate funding, juggling recessions and booms, trying to avoid bubble economies...not the structure for the future of the world.

This monetary policy is adequate in the U.S. and Europe because the diversity of private capital systems (old money) can carry the ball for long stretches of time and the fiscal system also forces expansion of new money through deficit spending. (See Chapter 3) But it's definitely not the 21st century paradigm.

In other countries, i.e. Asia, Russia and Eastern Europe, the lesser developed private systems can't counteract effectively in the inefficient and under-diversified monetary system. That's precisely why you read about all the currency problems.

Inadequacy of the world's monetary systems is one of the prime reasons governments (and individuals) do not have sufficient capital to bring about an abundant world.

EXPANSIVE FISCAL (no deficit)
EXPANSIVE MONETARY

This leaves us with the best doctrine: an *expansive monetary* system with a *relatively adequate* (balanced budget) *fiscal* system. This does not mean that government reduces its total spending. It means that government eliminates deficit spending. This is the appropriate economic structure for all sovereign nations — except in the dire circumstances of war and depression. **Unfortunately it cannot be implemented because our monetary disciplines are too anemic to generate an effective expansion of the money supply.**

This book covers the reasons why these systems are too underdeveloped and presents subsequent solutions so that 21st Century governments have more viable options to organize themselves appropriately. (See Chapter 16 for this restructuring.)

Except for war and economic crisis, fiscal policy should be based only on revenues received. Deficit spending is excessively inflationary. This is not to say that I always advocate a balanced budget. Considering the world's current deficient monetary system, I do not. We have already seen the effects of a restrictive monetary policy, hence we still need a substantial fiscal budget to overcome the major flaws of free market capitalism and an inadequate monetary system. Deficit spending also forces monetary expansion which causes some monetarization — the creation of new money.

As in the 1970's, trying to use monetary expansion to increase growth results in excessive inflation and any resultant growth is only marginal. The monetary system failed in the 70's by increasing the availability of new money without any direction — quantity instead of quality. There was probably too much new money issued on the demand side and the supply side (production) to enterprises and individuals without true need. For example, we over lent in successful industries, such as real estate and oil, causing over-capacity, and boom-and-bust scenarios. This narrow expansion resulted in an abundance of money chasing after limited goods and services.

History is chock full of these boom-and-bust economic periods. Economists refer to this as bubble economies.

Also, the current system of managing the economy has a tremendous inequity built into it. The supply of new money has been primarily controlled through interest rate fluctuations, and the larger capitalized industries can more easily withstand these higher interest costs. But these interest rate controls can hurt specific industries and smaller, less capitalized enterprises that really need new capital.

The 21st century economy can be efficiently stimulated through an expansive monetary policy. This policy must be implemented through a diversified monetary system, using equity as well as debt, focusing primarily on *new money that produces a variety of goods and services and develops natural resources.*

Businessmen and consumers won't borrow at any cost when the economy looks bad, so — as we saw in the 1930's and Japan in the 90's— cheap and easy debt doesn't stimulate borrowing on the commercial side.

This is one of the main reasons why some new money creation should be attached to equity financing (ownership-common stock), and not just debt. Equity financing has no debt service, therefore, businessmen are more willing to use this capital. Since cash flow and profit are unaffected, success is more likely. This encourages producers to add employees and increase capacity, bringing customers to the economy. When new money is infused into production it results in increased commercial activity, creates taxable profits and adds payroll tax revenue. This revenue feeds the fiscal system, allowing the necessary government spending to direct the country.

In truth, this burgeoning activity accelerates other commerce to increase production, resulting in even more tax revenues.

Additional expansion of the money supply has to be implemented for the production of goods and services. This does not mean that we eliminate the creation of money on the demand (consumer) side. Demand generally motivates businesses to expand, but nothing produces over-inflation more readily than excess end user money — consumer debt. Therefore, *additional excess* monetary expansion has to go to the supply side. (See Chapter 11)

Fiscal policy is used to help stimulate demand by the recirculation programs of a Federal government. Monetary policies should be used to stimulate production through a diversified monetary system. This is the formula for a healthy, thriving economy. One that creates sufficient velocity of circulation to result in enough money over time to accomplish all our humanitarian and economic goals.

$$E = mC^f$$

WHAT'S WRONG?

5 PROBLEMS WITH MONETARY SYSTEMS

I do want to take a little time and briefly go through the volatile history of monetary systems to depict the problems in recent years with the current systems — in countries, mature and immature, big and small.

LIST OF CENTRAL BANKING PROBLEMS

➤ *PROBLEM 1*

Germany's central monetary authority, the Bundstbank, is run by nationals who are consumed with the fear of hyper-inflation. Memories of the hyper-inflation collapse in the 1920's are still fresh in their minds. This short time frame has caused a very tight rein on monetary expansion. Unfortunately, this policy affects all of Europe and keeps German economy stifled with low growth and high unemployment. (Although, with a single delivery system, it is debatable that a looser policy would be more beneficial.)

➤ *PROBLEM 2*

Eastern European banks in almost every country have run into trouble during their transition to capitalism. **Hungary** has had to bail out state banks. The **Czech Republic** had a series of banking scandals and bust-ups that threatened a systemic collapse. In **Bulgaria,** a failure to reform has left banks with a collective negative net worth. **Estonia's** shimmering reputation has been recently tarnished by banking scandal — proving that cronyism and book-cooking do not necessarily stop at the country's borders. **Poland** has double digit inflation as of this writing.

I'll leave for another discussion the problems in the old **Soviet Union — Russia**, where many banks have faded into memory and the surviving banks control the bulk of privatized assets. The International Monetary Fund (IMF) is coming to the rescue again after the current collapse.

➤ PROBLEM 3
When the **Swedish** government deregulated banking in the mid-1980's, banks over lent indiscriminately to big industrial firms and real estate developers (another example of over-concentration and overlending). Losses almost wiped the banks out and forced the government to step in with a massive bailout.

➤ PROBLEM 4
Banks in **Latin America** have been typically accident prone. **Chile** suffered a devastating banking crisis in the early 1980's. The currency turmoil in **Mexico** at the end of 1994 came on top of banking over-expansion and careless lending binges. Mexico's banking mess is far from being resolved. Their banking system still has major problems today, even after the U.S. bailout. In **Argentina**, banking system customers drew out 40% of their deposits in early 1995. In 1994, more than half of **Venezuela's**

commercial banks needed a bail out. Several were nationalized or closed. **Bolivia** has had a complete hyper-inflationary collapse.

I won't even take the time to talk about **Brazil's** frenzied history of incredible hyper-inflationary failures.

➤ PROBLEM 5
Even the mighty growth economies of the Pacific Rim have run into problems. **Japan**, the economic powerhouse of the latter half of the 20th Century, has been brought to her knees economically by an under diversified system that allowed rapid expansion of money through low cost loans — causing undue speculation. Then, with no consensus about the consequences, the rug was rapidly pulled out! This collapsed the economy into deep recession. It still hasn't recovered and its financial-banking system is still racked with problems.

Most of the other **Pacific Rim** economies are slowing. **Thailand, Malaysia, Indonesia** and **Korea** are all facing economic collapse and need an economic bail out similar to Mexico. The Korean bank crisis was caused by a rash of overlending and defaults by a few big companies. Various bailouts have been proposed. The IMF has been forced to fill the breach. The **Philippines** is trying hard to control inflation without choking growth, but both the Philippines and Indonesia have seen a restructured devaluation of their currencies. In Indonesia, of more than 200 banks, only a mere handful are still solvent. A typical burst bubble economy has left the country in shambles. **Malaysian** bank loans seem to be failing and they might need a costly bailout to meet international capital requirements.

The daisy chain of financial crisis in the Pacific has been the direct result of easy money. Bank loans at comfortable interest rates allowed conglomerates in South Korea and Indonesia to expand and fortress market share without having to fret about payback. In Thailand and the Philippines, fixed exchange rates made foreign currency loans look like bargains. Trouble came when this easy money dried up. These aggressive companies with their new found debt burdens got stuck in the mud. Restructuring with its accompanying cutbacks and plant closures, only makes the mud thicker.

Even **Taiwan** is not entirely immune from these forces, but they seem to have found their way out of the muddy path and onto solid ground. True, their currency has undergone a modest devaluation and a tolerable decline in share prices, but economic growth stays strong. There are a number of reasons for this. Among them, Taiwan has a light foreign debt and better banking regulations than their neighbors. But the salient reason is worthy of replication. Taiwan has a more flexible economy than most other Asian countries and is therefore in a preferred place to handle crisis. In short, Taiwan makes it easy for new companies to get a start— and for old ones to fail. But, as this book is being published, they are having severe banking problems.

Mainland **China** had to recapitalize their four biggest state banks which accounts for nine tenths of all bank lending.

Australia has also been affected by the current Asian crisis. But their banking system is healthier after recovering from their reckless lending in the 1980's and a 10% inflation rate.

➤ PROBLEM 6

Asia. Central banks of **India** and **Turkey** have also had to devalue currency because of improper over-expansion of money. Turkey has one of the world's highest inflation rates and its current exchange is 280,000 lires to the dollar. As of this writing, **Pakistan** is in a state of crisis. Their rupees have plunged, creating a 25% gap between official exchange rate and the market rate.

➤ PROBLEM 7

In the last 10 years, banking crisis has hit 20 **African countries**, making it even more difficult economically and politically to enter into the 21st Century. Even **South Africa's** currency has seen substantial devaluation in recent times.

The International Monetary Fund (IMF) was established to mitigate these currency (monetary) problems, and currently, it's in the news on a daily basis. Concerns about their severe demands are definitely valid. For example, in South Korea, the IMF is currently requiring interest rates in the 20% range. This is 15% above the inflation rate. Spokesmen for the IMF claim that these high interest rates are necessary to harness inflation and restore confidence and that fiscal tightening (read budget-cutting) balances cut the cost of cleaning up the financial sector.

But the problem in East Asia stems from a wildly untenable financial system, not high inflation and fiscal extravagance. Tightening the money screws and squeezing fiscal policy makes the economy a step child. Banks and industrial companies with high debt load suffer even more. Companies bite the dust and the whole idea of shoring up the currency and increasing investor confidence becomes an illusion. Certainly, the economic screw needs turning, particularly on monetary policy, but the IMF might be too heavy-handed here. The policies of the IMF are a crisis-management — short term band-aid. $E=mCf$ is the long term cure.

The international picture gives a much clearer current view of the failure of commercial banking (new money) systems. **If implementation had been through many smaller — and varied institutions — you would see less corruption, less inept lending and more enterprises succeeding because of the reduction of debt servicing and higher equity participation.**

➤ PROBLEM 8

U.S. Historical. We've just looked at the current international situation, let's consider U.S. monetary issues. Here are just a few examples of the recent problems of having *one under-diversified system*: the S & L crisis; excessive oil patch loans; excessive international and individual loans; the Federal Reserve Board causing inflation and then missing the call to stem inflation (early 70's); then again missing the call by keeping interest rates too high for too long in the early 80's; the ultimately bad decision to tighten the supply in the early thirties, one of the more obvious causes of the Great Depression.

As a matter of fact, in our nation's first 150 years, among many other economic displacements, the immature monetary system and consequent lack of fiscal systems created the panics of 1837, 1857, 1873, 1893. 1907; the Banking Crisis of 1884; the recessions of 1892-6, 1904 and 1921; the severe depression from 1873 to 1879 and the Great Depression of the 1930's.

The ways things stand now, we're the laboratory rats, chasing each other's tails round and round in a vicious cycle. **The current single monetary (banking) system is too limited and too under-diversified in its infusion of money. This stifles growth, competition and employment. Therefore, the fiscal side of government — consciously or subconsciously — attempts to make up the slack with its programs and deficit spending.** Then, to cover its deficit spending, it mostly borrows money instead of printing it (monetarization). Consequently, the interest rate factor compounds the deficit.

Something here does not make sense. We need a total reorganization of the economics of federal governments. (See Chapter 16)

This is only a brief and partial list of the many problems with monetary policy and the inadequacies of systems throughout the world. I could go on and on but the purpose of this book is not to discuss the hundreds of examples highlighting the shortcomings of modern monetary systems.

$E=mCf$ is written to help solve these problems.

I strongly feel that world governments should be researching, discussing and finding better ways to handle their economic challenges. They should take more into account the frailties of human beings which a single institution — central organization — especially accentuates (This is depicted so vividly by the economic collapse of the Soviet Union).

Of course, we have suffered many domestic problems wherein the FRB has had to bail out large and small banks from their excesses. But in today's global economy, as well as the past, banking (monetary) systems are all intertwined. Small banks and countries borrow from large banks. Chain reactions happen (i.e., the recent Asian collapse).

Why have we seen so many failures — both current and historical — in global monetary systems? How could the economic structures of so many countries fall apart?

In truth, there are many reasons for these failures, such as over-corrections, mismanagement and political interferences, but these failings can be drastically reduced. How? Two major ways: **1) by having many systems deliver the funds, reducing the ravages of human error; 2) and by educating the public with full disclosure regarding monetary and financial functions.**

6 FLAWS OF CAPITALISM

Capitalism is a wonderful freedom-oriented and wealth-building system. Capitalism is the best system we have on earth. Capitalism is an economic system in which the means of production are privately owned. Business organizations produce goods for a market guided by the forces of supply and demand. Capitalism requires a financial system that enables business firms to borrow large sums of money, or capital, to maintain and expand production. Underlying capitalism is the presumption that private enterprise is the most efficient way to organize economic activity. Adam Smith expressed this idea in his Wealth of Nations (1776), extolling the free market in which the businessman is "led by an invisible hand to promote an end which was no part of his intention."

The marketplace is the center of the capitalist system. It determines what will be produced, who will produce it, and how the rewards of the economic process will be distributed. From a political standpoint, the market system has two distinct advantages over other ways of organizing the economy: (a) no person or combination of persons can easily control the marketplace, which means that power is diffuse and cannot be monopolized by a party or a clique; (b) the market system tends to reward efficiency with profits and to punish inefficiency with losses. Economists often speak of capitalism as a free-market system ruled by competition.

Having said this, we must face the fact that there are several flaws in a pure free market system, as in all human endeavors.

First, in a free enterprise structure, there is a continual, natural flow of capital to the powerful, more highly educated and already wealthy by various means, both legal and illegal. This natural concentration of wealth reduces both the number of businesses and individual consumers, eventually hurting commerce and society. **All studies, research and statistics, in the past, present or future, will validate this scenario.** Even in the booming US, many studies have shown that inequality has increased sharply over the past thirty years. This means that the natural goal of an enterprise is to attain monopoly status. This coincides well with the natural goals of many individuals to become as rich as possible! Controlling the market and increasing profit has got to be the focus of its behavior. This flaw has been recognized by both the right and the left. In 1890, the Republican party (with the support of industry) passed the Sherman Antitrust Act. Years later, the Democratic party started a policy of **redistribution of individual wealth**.

This flaw is even accentuated by Adam Smith, "capitalists left to their own devices would rather collude than compete." Thankfully, the anti-trust authorities in various nations help in increasing competition and broadening the base of the marketplace and capitalism.

Frankly, I think the word **"redistribution"** is the wrong word for this policy. It should be called **recirculation**. The vast majority of government spending is allocated domestically. **It is not hoarded so that its recipients can live on its return. Money is spread to more individuals, creating more consumers. *It is eventually spent* back into private enterprise which again creates wealth in certain capitalists, and to some extent, their workers. It creates *velocity of circulation* (turnover).**

The major risk to capitalism is that conservative or classical economic philosophers do not believe in this recirculation. By not believing, they hinder the improvement of effective recirculation programs, thus placing capitalistic societies in danger from economic depression or outright revolution.

A second flaw is the *obsession with immediate maximizing of profit*. Private capital and management are constantly expecting relatively quick and high rates of returns. Public capital is more of a long term venture and not so profit-oriented, so it works more for the benefit of all of society, including business. Consequently, we see public investment in infrastructure, education, research and other necessary projects.

For example, as we become an efficient high tech society, millions of the current service workers could be displaced. We might need increased public capital to provide additional employment and community services for these people. Of course, this will keep these displaced individuals as effective consumers which continues to stimulate economic well being.

The current Asian crisis is another example of this flaw. They have not developed an effective consumer base and are relying too much on exports to fuel their growth.

The truth is, as capitalism gets more efficient it generally requires less labor to produce all the needed goods and services. Which, of course, means less customers. Thus far, capitalism has solved this problem through innovation and the creation of new goods and services (some of which didn't even exist a few years ago). But successful capitalism still might mean larger governmental involvement (fiscal and monetary) in order to fund a more wide-spread abundance. I strongly recommend increases in the use of monetary systems more than the fiscal systems.

The third flaw which should concern us all centers on the *challenge of running a business* (microeconomics) *with a customer base drawn from a fully employed and adequately compensated work force* (macroeconomics).

The natural inclination of a business owner is to either minimize his labor force or pay less for labor so he can make more profit. The current corporate downsizing and offshore flight to cheap labor markets provides classic examples of this behavior. Granted, these are correct business decisions for increasing profit. But, if all businesses in the economy implemented these policies, their sales would retreat drastically because their customers would not be well-paid enough to buy goods and services. This is one of the major problems for developing economies.

Conversely, when mass production is accompanied by mass consumption, a more evenly spread distribution of wealth occurs. Since this wealth is tied to production *and* consumption, the economy thrives.

In the general global economic debate, especially after the fall of communism, we hear very little of the flaws of capitalism and pure, free market systems. But these flaws definitely exist and it is important for public and private institutions alike to help overcome them if we want to expand our future on this planet. I hate to hear the words "we can't afford it." We can't afford to cure cancer, we can't afford to discover the mysteries of the oceans, we can't afford to explore the solar system.

We *can* afford it! Understanding the flaws of capitalism and getting our monetary system back on course can provide the capital to do it all!

Towards this end, **ONE OF THE MAJOR MISSIONS OF A FEDERAL GOVERNMENT HAS TO BE MACROECONOMIC WELL BEING.** Government funded programs, such as education, unemployment compensation, labor unions and laws, wage-protecting tariffs, and minimum wages are a necessity. Even military spending has proven to be an effective means of recirculation. But the vigorous policy of a government can also promote private solutions to this conflict. Private philanthropic measures can be encouraged, as can pension programs, profit sharing plans, esop, stock options, equity sharing policies, job training, child care and medical insurance. Even inflation is a way of compensating for this flaw! (See Chapter 9)

In fact, the exodus of private corporations to cheap foreign labor markets highlights the conflict between quick profit and the long-term good of the culture. Many of these foreign countries pay such low wages (or engage in slave labor), that they fail to produce a strong consumer base — one of the major reasons for the current Asian problem. This creates global overcapacity which is currently being funded by the U.S. consumer (trade deficit). When this stops, these nations could undergo serious recession. We see these conditions of over capacity (supply) throughout our history and in every part of the world. **If you don't give labor a spendable wage you won't have enough customers.**

Case in point: if we had dictatorial control over global production, several of the most productive nations could provide the bulk of goods and services for the rest of the world. Unfortunately, the rest of us would be unemployed and unable to purchase anything!

Admittedly, these fiscal and private policies are not the complete answer to this conflict, nor have we yet developed truly effective solutions. The continual political struggle to have the correct recirculation and balanced fiscal policy is the subject for another book.

Another flaw of capitalism is the intensification of competition. Competition is good, but over-competition can theoretically increase the capacity to such an extent that the price of goods and services is too drastically reduced and all the producers go bankrupt. This flaw is less impactful than the preceding two flaws and will not be covered in this book.

The main point with these flaws is this: *government is needed as a macroeconomic force to regulate commerce, recirculate wealth and have a competent monetary system.*

THE ECONOMIC RIGHT AND LEFT

Current congressional debate masks the basic philosophical differences of the two parties. The Right desires a pure "Laissez Faire" free market (classical) economic system as practiced from 1865 to 1932. (Which, by the way, led to inordinate recessions, a great depression, panics and an excessively large poor working class. See Chapter 5.) They believe there should be little or no government involvement in commerce. They contend that private enterprise, left alone, will solve most of society's problems.

This economic philosophy is dead wrong and has been proven so many times over the last century.

The Left desires an effective macroeconomic policy, but they attempt to implement it with government bureaucracies and an excessive fiscal policy (budget deficits).

These basic philosophical differences have stifled the political process.

I want to see the Right abandon their classical "Laissez Faire" policy and join with the Left in advocating governmental regulation and the recirculation of wealth. The debate should be centered on selecting appropriate government programs and improving operations, not on wiping them out.

I want to see the Left abandon their bureaucratic mentality, and start implementing more through private enterprise, similar to the symbiotic governmental relationship with the military industrial complex. If private enterprise is more efficient than government, there will be more fiscal funds available for other programs.

More importantly, I want both parties to finance some of their policies with a balanced budget and through an expansive, diversified, non-excessive, *inflationary monetary system.*

7 PROBLEMS AND LIMITATIONS OF ONE SYSTEM

The last half of the 20th century has seen an explosion of human endeavor. We've gone to the moon, cured diseases, ended the cold war, and hopped aboard the technology bullet train. Economically, unprecedented benefits have resulted from a well developed free enterprise system. Now, as we attempt to gracefully glide into the third millennium, we have a grand opportunity to continue our successful experiment by spreading democratic capitalism to more and more people throughout the world.

Unfortunately, we are trying to accomplish this task with one of the major economic powers quagmired in an archaic structure, developed over the centuries, not at all suitable to usher us into a prosperous new age.

Right now in the world, there is one, and only one system, to determine how much new money is created, who receives it and how it is controlled. To add to the mishmash, new money is created only through debt instruments. This is a very limiting and narrow way to adequately provide the capital needs of a vast and expansive 21st century economy.

The current monetary supply is mainly expanded by debt (bank loans). Only the commercial banking system significantly delivers new money into the system. Moreover, **most loans can only be received if you**

don't need them or you already have all the capital (collateral) you can use!

New money is infused into the economy solely through the use of debt instruments. Again, this not only limits who receives the funds, but it also spawns an excessive debt structure with significant psychological negatives. This is unwarranted. There should be an additional system that introduces money through equity (see Chapter 14). The consequence will be diversity and added direction to the infusion of money, without the negative cash flow strains of charging interest.

Monetary supply is partially controlled by interest rate fluctuation. These interest rates reflect the cost of capital, and for business people, interest — along with the price of labor and raw materials — directly affects pricing decisions. Consequently, increases in interest rates continually add to inflation until finally, the economy is reversed into deflation, causing a recession or depression.

This broad-brush approach also diminishes the availability of capital for production, hampering employment and growth. Excessive interest rates can also have a more direct, depressing effect on certain industries, such as housing and construction — which are vitally needed for the good of the population.

As the banking (monetary) system expands, the more successful companies and individuals can qualify for increasing new credit. This narrows the availability of easy money (credit). Eventually there is no real business reason (demand) for this capital and it results in over-expansion and speculation.

At this point the central banks substantially reduce or eliminate this credit by restricting availability and/or increasing price (interest rates), eventually causing economic contraction (recession-depression-deflation). Then it becomes even harder to pay back the loans which results in defaults and puts the entire banking system in jeopardy.

In actuality, the money supply is controlled by many forces simultaneously. No single agent controls it absolutely, including central banks. In fact, when central banks try to reduce the supply of money by raising interest rates, it can cause many debtors to pay off their loans faster which destroys new money. Moreover, in a downturn, new money is not created fast enough, which just compounds the economic downturn.

Does this paradoxical chain of events (process) make any sense?

BANK FAILURES

Since 1980, more than 100 poor countries — ranging from Argentina to Zaire — have suffered one or more banking crisis. (See Chapter 5) The cost of dealing with these setbacks is well over a half trillion dollars. Many of these countries have had to allocate the equivalent of more than a tenth of their annual GDP to nursing sick banks back or to health or closing them down.

There is no single cause for these bank breakdowns. Failure involves a combination of factors: economic volatility, shoddy management, weak regulation, political meddling, dubious loans (often to favorite shareholders), reckless lending.

Also, many of these nations do not have the well-developed non-banking capital markets and a sophisticated fiscal system like the U.S. that provide an alternative source of capital to the commercial banks. Consequently, these banking breakdowns are more devastating to their economies, exposing an even greater need to diversify than larger, richer countries.

General guidelines and international supervision can be established. Various reforms will help. But relying on one institution — commercial banking — as the sole provider of new money and the only source of new capital is to beg for disaster. The countries need many smaller institutions to create diversity, to spread the risk of failure. Of course, this still offers no absolute guarantee, but spreading the power definitely diffuses the danger.

Even though I am writing this book using references to the U.S. monetary system, my current critique regards all sovereign monetary systems. In fact, the U.S. Central bank — the Federal Reserve system — is probably the most adequately run in the entire world. One can only assume that my theory would progress even more quickly in less successful national monetary systems and will probably start there. (Current examples of the limitation of one system are well illustrated by monetary failures in Japan, Mexico, Indonesia, Russia. See Chapter 5.)

When all the potential buyers in an economy want more money and credit than a central bank thinks is healthy, the central bank refuses to supply the demand and that drives up interest rates. The higher interest rates depress the public's appetite for spending and the demand for new loans subsides.

The growth of money slows down.

On the surface, this approach seems universal and discreet, imposing the same discipline on all economic players equally — favoring none.

Unfortunately, it does not work that way! Higher interest rates punish the weakest and smaller players first and most severely. They also punish those industries mostly tied to debt financing.

Many family businesses and financial institutions are compelled to alter their behavior swiftly — raise prices, cut costs, borrow more to pay back higher interest costs. But others — usually the largest, more powerful, wealthier enterprises and individuals — and the largest commercial banks — are privileged to continue business as usual.

Is it written somewhere by the great economics god that high interest rates should fall unevenly on citizens and their enterprises? Why should the pain inflicted by seemingly equitable legislation be dependent on a company's income and profit levels? This fact is even exacerbated by archaic tax codes that allow uneven deductibility of interest expenses, again favoring larger business entities.

The real cost of higher interest rates places different burdens on the citizenry. The wealthiest and most successful suffer least; struggling businesses and lower-end families pay the premium. This culprit is Federal Reserve policy and the way in which high interest rates interact with the U.S. tax code. All taxpayers are allowed to deduct interest payments from their taxable incomes, but these deductions naturally became more valuable if one is in a higher-income bracket and is taxed at a high rate. In the current arrangement, a corporation saves approximately 40 percent of its interest costs on its tax bill. A wealthy individual, paying the maximum tax rate, recovers about 40-50 percent of his interest payments in tax savings. This effectively cuts the real cost of higher interest rates in half for them — while others pay full freight. **This differential is always present, but it becomes greatly magnified as interest rates rise.**

The consequence of rationing money only by price (interest rates) is unequivocal: new money is allocated, not by market forces or need, but according to the financial girth of prospective borrowers.

These high net worth borrowers can more easily overcome the cost of new money (credit) which means the central banks' ability to control new money through increases in interest rates becomes less effective. Consequently, they raise rates higher, which squeezes the lower end of the wealth spectrum even more, causing unnecessary financial and personal hardship. Moreover, when the going gets tough, larger multinational enterprises can completely side-step these high interest charges by borrowing from international banks at lower rates.

This process aggravates one of the major flaws of capitalism: "the poor get poorer, the rich get richer." (See Chapter 6) Higher interest rates cause more and more individuals to file for bankruptcy and in the end, the high-side survivors buy up the smaller, less healthy, contracting enterprises, consolidating wealth even further.

Central banks were created to prevent short term liquidity crises that could wipe out otherwise solvent banks. The Fed's architects call it elastic currency — a money supply that could grow or shrink flexibly in accordance with the fluctuating credit demands of the nation.

In a growth economy, there is always a demand for credit. The key question in this formula is "where should this credit go?" Unfortunately, history has proven both nationally and internationally, that its use is over-concentrated, which leads to boom-and-bust scenarios.

A vastly diversified delivery system — rather than one single system — will reduce these effects by directing new money credit to many different regions, for a variety of industries and uses.

In the U.S., the borrower's objective is to persuade the lender to provide the largest loan at the lowest price. The lender's job is to investigate whether the borrower is telling the truth and to monitor the borrower to make sure he lives up to his promises. The relationship is adversarial; increasingly, borrowers are trying to find legal dodges for repayment even when they have the money.

Equity lending instead of debt lending substantially reduces this adversarial role and creates a sense of partnership, in which repayment comes more from profit sharing, not from variable interest rate charges.

USURY

In the not-too-distant past, certain principles of money were not subject to alteration by society's money managers. They might be ignored or forgotten for a time, but they could not be repealed. One of these principles was the ancient biblical injunction against usury. The definition of usury may have vacillated over the centuries, but the moral meaning was the same. When lenders insisted on terms that were sure to ruin the borrowers, this was wrong. This was usury.

There were practical, as well as moral reasons, why usury was considered a sin. It was more than a social plea for fairness or generosity from the wealthy. No social system could tolerate usury, not as a permanent condition, because it led to an economic life that was self-devouring. The money monger collected his due until he owned all the property and the peasants had nothing. No one would really survive. Who would buy from the money monger if he had all the money? And what kind of life would the peasants have?

CONCLUSION

In the U.S., we slowly worked our way out of the Great Depression of the 30's and the high inflation of the 70's. Now, I suspect that most experts think that our country has a fairly comprehensive and well rounded family of theories to guide monetary policy. I hope I'm wrong, but I expect that one of these years another major economic problem will arise to plague us. At that time we will discover that the prevailing monetary theory and operations are not able to handle crisis well. We definitely see it right now in many other countries around the world.

We're currently seeing examples of this breakdown in other parts of the world. If we study the Asian catastrophes of the 90's, we can easily see how the flaws of these monolithic systems have almost totally tumbled their economies. These countries feature a capitalism based on cronyism, familism and corruption, and are ruled by economic combines. These government, bank and business cliques get together to decide who gets contracts and how they are split. They determine who gets loans, at what rate, and with what collateral. For what they do every day, in America they would all be in pinstriped prison suits, not pinstriped business suits.

When crisis does happen, relying on existing economic theory and a single developing system, the central bank will misdiagnose the new problem and we will have another financial bubble or squeeze.

We are not perfect in practice or theory, therefore the delivery system has to be diversified to reduce the severity of any wrong decisions.

8 STATISTICS AND FORMULAS

"There are three kinds of economists:
those who can count and those who can't."
OLD ECONOMICS JOKE

It is a truism that economists spend a bulk of their time squeezing statistics through computer models and their formulas, then using them to justify policy. The problem is that they concern themselves too little with the reliability of their sacred numbers. This is the big glitch of economics. Traditional ways to measure economic activity are losing their water. This is not just an issue to be debated by scholars. Erroneous figures mislead the populace. The weekly Economist magazine devotes a column in most issues to statistical abuse.

More to the point: as these time-weathered measures become less reliable, policy makers and financial institutions are placing more and more weight on them.

These statistics and formulas fatally impact the quality of our daily lives. The government's numbers don't stop at merely distorting the statistics; they actually distort the economy. They hinder us from reaching the next height in capitalism.

You see, economists love to use their statistics to bolster their myriad philosophies. For example, since 1970 the Fed has utilized elaborate econometric models to try to forecast the effects of monetary policy and other influences on the American economy. These computer models spring from a series of fascinating mathematical equations, with a slew of variables and theoretical consequences. The Fed's computer model in Washington has become more and more sophisticated, eventually utilizing more than 160 equations.

It has been proven time and time again — for example, during the roller coaster period of the late 70's, early 80's and the boom of the late 90's — that statistics and models cannot be counted on to accurately predict an outcome as complicated as the environment of the economy. Economic forecasts produced by feeding numbers into complex models are notoriously bad at predicting turning points because they tend to extrapolate the recent past. Still, economists hide behind them.

And they still can't predict economical reality with any kind of certainty.

Piloting human commerce by relying strictly on statistics is like steering an airplane by only reading a map. At best, economic statistics are general guides — usually inaccurate — and they give a false description of the well-being of the populace. Notice how economists like to debate in esoteric language, and hide behind mountains of monetary statistics, instead of talking about material goals and social equity. Worse, non-economists are bullied into silence by these imperious economists. The language of their sonorous debates regarding their fractious, competing theories is all-but-impenetrable to the layman.

There have been many errors by economists in this century who have been trying to reach a specific growth rate, a particular monetary supply number, an inflation rate, a modicum of productivity, a certain capacity utilization, or any number of macroeconomic sign posts.

Hopefully, we can learn from history. We can see that there have been numerous inconsistencies, gross errors in calculations, confusion regarding the meanings, and disagreement as to the causes. The result is a great deal of misinformation and counterproductive action. In particular, economists have to be careful not to fit the world into their theories but to adjust their theories to the realities around them. You can read one economist and get one view, read another and be treated to an entirely opposite perspective. As always the real world is more complicated than statistics suggest.

INFLATION AS A GUIDE

Through the years, economists have relied on their pet mathematical formulas to measure and operate the monetary system. This is absolute folly. No matter how sophisticated these formulas, no matter how accurate, it is **impossible to operate and balance mathematically an operational delivery system that is so huge and narrow that it is intrinsically flawed.** It is a human system, not an absolute physical science system.

Economics is a social discipline, it deals with the behavior of people and human institutions. The social universe has no "natural laws" as the physical sciences do. Therefore it is subject to continuous change. This means that assumptions that were valid yesterday can become invalid and totally misleading in no time at all.

Economists base their models on a tidy world with a too-simple view of psychology. Economists need to deal with the genetically-based neural wiring that predisposes animals and humans in certain ways. Until economists take these humans factors more into account, they won't have much luck in predicting economic events and behaviors.

The usual assumption is that people just want more of whatever it is. It may be that people will deviate powerfully from classical economic models if given opportunities and choices. Because economists don't factor in human nature enough, we are deprived of a wider variety of choices.

Monetary predictions, theories and formulas have also failed miserably. Basically, they try to measure and control the entire stock of the money supply and the demand for it. But they don't take into account where the money is going or how it is being used **(quantity versus quality)**.

In an extensively diversified monetary delivery system, the only statistic that is vitally important is inflation and the information needed to stop any excess inflationary spiral. As a starting point, we would specify a *range not a specific target* and utilize several different types of formulas to calculate our progress.

The discipline of economics has come up with various and sundry theories and definitions for growth, productivity, savings and the like. Unfortunately, this is only the beginning. Economists love their little theories. There will always be a new one to throw into the

$$E = mC^f$$

pot. **To narrowcast a massive economy through a single definition of growth and its statistical counterpart would only *limit* human economic potential and any inherent progressive benefit.**

Gathering numbers describing the commerce of 6 billion people is probably an impossible task at this (or any) time. It is desirable to have some form of measurement, but trying to control economies based on numbers that pop out of a formula can and has been disastrous. Economics is not an absolute physical science system, it is a human system! Moreover, far too many statisticians measure output in the 19th century definition rather than that of the 21st.

Three trends pose difficult challenges to traditional statistics: (1) globalization (2) the information age — invisibility (production of non-physical goods) (3) technological advancement. These vital factors all but make some standard statistical measures useless. Figures on the production of beans, bread and bombers are at our fingertips, but more useful data about today's fastest growing industries— computing, telecommunications, business services and finance — are much harder to come by. These activities are mostly invisible and difficult to assign targeting numbers.

The real problem is that economists attempt to describe growth by arriving at their hallowed statistics and inserting them in their sacred formulae. Unfortunately, there is no agreement on *what growth is* or how it is adequately attained, or even at what level it should be. There is even a new calculation called the "human development" index, an option to the GDP (Gross Domestic Product). Here's an example to boggle your mind. The Growth rate is currently 2.8%. Based on the GDP, their hallowed statistics and formulas, the Fed says it should be 4%. How can you limit the economic health of human beings!? Pointless! The definition of growth is unattainable and the statistic of growth can never be accurate, so why bother? (See Chapters 9 and 14) Unfortunately, most current macroeconomic monetary theory prefers rules based on these statistics. It can only be a very general guide post, not a specifically structured goal. These misguided beliefs, which tie the growth of monetary supply to a percentage of GNP (Gross Natural Product) — or any other general statistic — only limit the human economic condition and our evolution into the next level of capitalism.

The current definition of growth is definitely too statistically narrow. Some economists believe we are producing too much waste simply to satisfy the need to produce this definition of growth.

Others believe that many are taking our natural resources, consuming too many material goods. The definition of growth has to be broadened as regarding what it means by *services* which do not take up natural resources.

I am an optimist. I believe in the ingenuity of mankind to overcome its problems and continue to progress, that human and natural resources are unlimited, that high prices caused by shortages will encourage the search for new supplies or alternatives.

In plain language, **if the fiscal and monetary systems are relatively efficient, they will support massive growth and favor human economic structures with unlimited potential. There's no need for "have** nots" in the proper capitalistic paradigm, only ones that "have more".

There's a lot of discourse in the marketplace from folks who want to achieve a 0% inflation rate. Of course, that assumes that human beings (commerce) and their measurements are perfect. Is this absurd or what? Human capitalistic endeavors will never be perfect. There will be bankruptcies and failures, reducing goods and services, and consequently creating some form of inflation in the issuance of new money. This is inevitable.

Of course, we don't want deflation either. This usually brings with it recession, depression and consequent suffering and hardship. Here's the bottom line: *an inflation range has to be developed within a healthy range, avoiding both deflation and excess inflation.*

The point is, we can have unlimited growth if we're not restricted to any specific definition. Only excess inflation has to be controlled. (See chapter 12.)

9 INFLATION VERSUS GROWTH

Inflation versus growth is always a highly debated topic among politicians, writers and economists. I hereby throw my two cents into the ring.

This is very simple, really. **In an overall economy, the only thing that creates excess inflation is *too much money chasing* an inadequate supply of purchasable goods and services.** This is proved whenever the overall supply of money is reduced (or even eliminated). Prices come down. Conversely, increase the money supply and prices creep back up the ladder.

My book is basically structured around pure economic reason. I don't want to make moral or humanitarian judgments (although they are tempting). But let me break from this discipline just once. *To reduce jobs and growth simply to attain zero inflation is not only economically wrong but morally repugnant.* Let me state it loud and clear: it is irresponsible to make people suffer economically — and therefore physically, mentally and emotionally — because of an error in the system of delivery.

There is a very strong, almost one-to-one, long-term relationship between money supply growth and inflation. This relationship holds for all countries and time periods. Rarely do we find such strong evidence in economics. Attempts to fuel alternative explanations of excess inflation — such as high capacity utilization rates or wage growth — are just not substantiated on an overall macroeconomic level. It is a government phenomenon!

This is again being currently proven in the United States in the late 1990's as growth expands without inflation. Moreover, with diverse and gradually implemented monetary delivery systems, we can foster even faster growth without excess inflation.

You see, the main reason excess inflation is historically tied to excess growth is the nature of the monetary system itself. Under the current structure, monetary expansion is predicated on the ability of consumers (and producers) to borrow more money. The better they are doing economically, the more money they can borrow. **WHETHER THEY NEED IT OR NOT!**

Consequently, excess borrowing by already successful producers and consumers, expands the monetary supply too narrowly without true need. This causes a cycle of short-term successes, followed by a demand for increased wages, etc. This is the vicious cycle of blindside economics.

Efficient and diversified monetary expansion should break this stagnant growth philosophy and control excess inflation.

In our current philosophy, the business cycle is married to the monetary cycle, which is the major cause of ups and downs.

Frankly, I believe the term "business cycle" is a misnomer. It should be labeled the monetary cycle, not the business cycle. A boom-and-bust macroeconomic cycle — rapidly expanding, then contracting — is really caused by a singular monetary delivery system. Excess capital (new money) is delivered to already successful industries and/or individuals until they over-expand — BOOM — then the monetary system contracts *even in those industries* where over-capitalization did not occur — BUST!

INFLATION

In every era of economic history, the rhetoric of the time concerns itself with "hard money" or "easy money", falling prices or rising prices, inflation or deflation. In truth, these debates are really focused on which economic class must suffer, on creditors and debtors, and which configuration would benefit the wealthy or the producers.

American politicos have yearned for a golden resting point, an all-too-elusive state of neutrality between "price stability" and "zero inflation". They proffer pipe dreams of an economic utopia where neither class gains at the expense of the other. In actual fact, neutral money has rarely been realized. We cannot control the actions of the entire human race to attain a mythical zero point inflation.

Moreover, the idea of neutral money sounds good; a strong. stable social order would seem to be the end result. The opposite it actually true. So called "stable money" would only create disorder. In the real world, stable money has only fed an hysteria of privilege and advantage. Certain economic interests operated without shackles, able to raise prices and wages at will. Others were anchored to steady decline, doomed to fail if the situation persisted.

In the 1920s and later in the 1980s, the myth of "stable money" was a cornerstone of democratic capitalism. Economists lulled people into a false sense of security. we were led to believe that a stable dollar offered no artificial advantage to anyone. Hard working people were relieved to see that the stigma of rising prices was obfuscated. Also, in trying to attain stable money — or zero percent inflation — this objective cannot be effectively measured, monitored or enforced, mainly because of the long lag time from the issuance of increases in the new money. If the monetary authorities make an error on the side of contraction, it usually causes declining prices, recession, and sometimes, depression. **Remember, all this results in human hardship.**

The point is, *there must be some inflation.* The question is how much? The question becomes even more important when one considers the dire consequences of deflation. Our planet's record with unstable money — which includes the experience of the U.S. — was not an aberration of history. Cycles of pure inflation and deflation were recurring in the world's commerce long before there was a United States. They appeared in capitalist economies regardless of whether the currency was gold, silver, copper or a combination of those metals. Inflation occurred regularly, both when governments managed money or when it was totally controlled by the market forces of private enterprise; with or without central banks.

And in our modern day economies, many of the debtors are also equity players who prosper in a growth economy. Add to this that debit instruments have also been altered to offset the ravages of inflation. Growth has to win out and growth with a diversified monetary delivery system can rapidly progress without excess inflation.

EXCESS INFLATION

The fact is: *real economic growth* is never inflationary. Inflation is caused by too *rapid growth* in the money supply. For example, when the U.S. economy grows three percent a year there are three percent more goods and services that people can buy. People need additional dollars to make these purchases. Allowing the supply of dollars to grow by three percent a year just matches the additional goods and services available. Prices feel no need to rise. Inflation can only occur if the money supply grows by more than three percent a year. This assumes one can measure growth?!

A successful economy should always have some inflation. Inflation is the natural result of the imperfect use of new money creation and the inability to measure real growth. Since we're not perfect, inflation will always be with us. We definitely do not want deflation, which usually results in unemployment, deep recession / depression and human hardship. **What we need to avoid is *excess* inflation, not inflation itself**. Since any number one chooses can describe excessive inflation, I will call it any amount above 4-5%. (See Chapter 12)

What does inflation do? Inflation redistributes wealth from creditors to debtors, from those who have excess to those who have none. It takes the most from those who have the largest accumulations of surplus (wealth) but because of their size does not subject them to real suffering. They are not impoverished, merely made less wealthy. In inflationary times, the wealthy are also able to adjust with variable interest charges and other flexible instruments.

Inflation damages well fixed families by eroding the value of their accumulated financial assets, but inflation also spreads wealth widely — enabling the broad middle class to enjoy a higher standard of living and to acquire greater net worth. They do this largely through borrowing and repaying their debts in depreciated dollars. Of course, they spent this wealth in cumulative goods and services, which eventually expands the wealth of the capitalists.

Deflation reverses the process. Anyone who owns credit assets automatically enjoys greater wealth as prices fall. Their dollar assets purchase more in real goods, the value of their accumulated capital steadily increases. Left with little or no savings, debtors depending solely on their own productive labor and credit for their livelihoods see their incomes shrink and the real burdens of their debts grow larger. "The rich got richer, the poor got poorer." (For one of the major flaws of capitalism, see Chapter 6.)

Of course, when *monetary deflation* happens — caused by contracting money supply — prices, spending, demand and growth decline, which hurts overall commerce and increases human hardship.

Conversely, excess inflation takes too much of a toll and creates disharmony in the economy.

The central banking systems seem to be deathly afraid of the "I" word. Whatever their reasons, their major policy is to subdue inflation at any cost. Granted, inflation can always be reduced by depressing or killing the economy and unemploying people. **Still, the notion that growth and employment should be stifled to reduce inflation is absolutely**

ridiculous. Additionally, over fine-tuning the inflation rate by having a goal of 0%-1% could lead to conditions of deflation-recession, because this misses the mark on the side of deflation.

Inflation wipes out errors in the human/capitalistic system. There will always be errors in the delivery of new and old money. A low amount of inflation will allow for additional, efficient expansion and offset some of the ravages of a marketplace and the flaws of capitalists.

The antidote is some form of lower inflation, which helps solve one of the major flaws in capitalism: the over concentration of wealth in the hands of the wealthy! (See Chapter 6) Recession-depression (deflation) encourages consolidation of ownership — which only accentuates the flaw.

HOW TO IMPROVE

<u>10</u> WHY DIVERSIFY THE MONETARY DELIVERY SYSTEMS?

In almost every country in the world, we have already witnessed numerous failures of centralized banking systems. **There is no way to prove my doctrine though sample testing, mathematical formulas or econometrics.** The only way would be to implement diversification in an existing country. Therefore, the following reasons will hopefully convince the skeptics why we have to have a diversity of monetary delivery systems.

1. *Diversification reduces banking favoritism* (**paying off buddies and giving loans to friends**), **nepotism, bribes, political cronyism, shoddy management and criminal activity. At the very least, it decreases the negative effects of these actions. Insider allocation of "new money" is used for ego gratification instead of a productive-needed use.**

2. The *boom-bust scenario* we see in various assets, industries and countries will be greatly *reduced* by not over lending in successful industries and individuals. It makes managing risks less difficult! It reduces the effect of the unpredictable delay between changes and interest rates

and their subsequent influences on the economy.

3. *Diversification gives more capitalistic opportunities to others* — creating more capitalists (business owners) and increasing competition. It also brings more individuals and enterprises into the capitalistic system. The current system favors large banks and rich customers. *Diversity spreads the new money around* — creating other capitalistic opportunities at the same time reducing human hardship.

4. The major *reason for business failure is lack of capital,* not competition or mismanagement.

5. **Diversification expands credit based on the ability to succeed and not just on the ability to repay. Distribution of new money (loans) should also be based on the quality of your talent and need for your enterprise (commerce) not just the quantity of your collateral.**

6. *Diversification dilutes the power that any one system brings to monetary creation.* Absolute power corrupts absolutely. Why should only one financial institution — commercial banking have the monopolistic power of monetary creation and infusion?

7. *Diversification reduces the effects of any errors of monetary distribution during expansion or contraction.* With diversity, during a contraction — it will not hurt certain industries which do not need less expansion. For example, let's say that the monetary authorities want less new money in the economy. At the same time, we still need new housing in our society. Consequently, a separate system will still provide funding at reasonable rates for building and buying homes.

Diversification allows for errors on the monetary expansion/inflation side of the equation rather than the contraction side. The end result is a lesser chance of recession/depression.

8. *Excessive wide range defaults and bankruptcies will not hurt the new money delivery systems* as much because it's spread among many systems rather than a single banking system. Therefore, the monetary system will have less stress due to economic volatility.

9. Granted, the regulation of a very large, single system has its challenges, but *a diversity of systems allows decision markers to more effectively reduce the over-lending to a particular individual, company, industry or geographical area.* The dilemma of regulation is that it's very hard to deal with things when life is good. Who tells the banks not to lend to energy when energy is the hottest part of the economy and running up great profits? Or shipping? Or real estate? Having other delivery systems with different objectives will more effectively control over-lending, thereby reducing boom/bust scenarios within an industry and an entire economy.

10. *Diversity also helps control the amounts used for aggregate demand stimulation and supply creation,* depending on the needs of each. Having more control of the quality and quantity of new money being issued results in less of a chance of an over-expansive money supply creating a bubble economy.

11. *Diversity can provide more capital to arenas with high need,* such as low tech industries and lower income areas.

12. Monetary policy is an art not a science! Monetary policy requires judgment at every stage of the process, from the initial formulation to the final implementation. Judgment is susceptible to human error. If there is an error in one major system it can lead to tragic consequences. *But several errors in a multiplicity of systems can be much more easily overcome.*

13. In the carrying out of monetary policy, there is debate regarding having set operating rules versus management discretion. Because of statistical inaccuracies and the unknown future, designing a contingency rule for all currently conceivable possibilities is too costly to implement and all-but-impossible. As a consequence, all central bank policies are dependent on human judgment in some form or another. *The more diversified the delivery system, the less a judgment error by central banking management will result in catastrophe.*

14. **The fiscal system operates on a very diversified level. There are many governments in the fiscal system – Federal, State, County, City. Within those governments there are many delivery systems — military, Medicare, welfare (social and corporate), Social Security, education — resulting in less catastrophes. Also old money operates at a very diversified level.** Why shouldn't new money? Prior to the Great Depression, old money was less diversified, which resulted in severe economic troughs.

15. Credit risk formulas and models of commercial banks, which are inherently flawed, will be reduced in consequence because money creation is moved to other institutions. Improving and increasing regulation and risk models can help — but it's not the answer. *Reckless lending will be scattered and there will be*

fewer defaults with the use of equity rather than all debt financing.

16. A key element in the art of monetary policy is *coping with change*. The current, most important change that central banks face is the globalization of monetary policy. Again, *with more decision makers and more diversified delivery systems, the monetary brokers will find it easier and safer to cope with these changes.*

17. *We need diversity to reduce the negative effects of excess greed.* All you have to do is watch TV or read a newspaper to recognize that the frailties, mistakes, and ethical turpitude of human beings are realities that allow bad things to happen. These moral shortcomings can be epitomized in one word: *greed*...both legal and illegal.

Illegal greed is an action that the law has to prevent. Theoretically, if lawbreakers are prosecuted vigorously enough, would-be cheats decide it's not worth the risk. This idea works much better in theory than in practice. Case in point: widespread S&L criminal activity. A more adequate prevention can be found in a diversified system wherein the effects of illegal activity are minimized.

Legal greed — unethical activity of one kind or another — is something altogether different. The business of selfish interest can be seen as both a virtue and a vice. The desire to earn provides the incentive for a host of market activities in the first place, but too much greed weakens the system. Like it or not, legal greed is one of the flaws of capitalism. (See Chapter 6) Again, diversity reduces the effects of this flaw.

Since the pre-Civil War free banking era, we haven't had to worry about this so much in the U.S. But in Russia we can see vividly the flaw that lack of diversity can create. This flaw is exacerbated when a country loses confidence in its currency and ownership is concentrated in the banks with the power of monetary creation.

18. The U.S. Federal Reserve System has many checks and balances to offset factors of self-interest and other human frailties. But *with the delivery basically in one system, any errors that do get through are certainly overly exaggerated.*

19. Our single banking system is less and less willing to share risk. Yet, risk is critical to the progress of the private sector and hence to economic growth. *Our single system has lost the ability to foster the development of novel or unstandardized – in short, risky — private enterprise.* This means that economic development slows and future generations are disadvantaged. Currently, Americans are borrowing ever more from foreigners to finance spending and investment at home. This is fueled by our country's economic boom. Doesn't this seem odd to you? Why is it necessary for our economy to borrow abroad. Is it possibly because the current monetary system is inadequate?

If we had many systems delivering new money, several could be designated to provide such risk capital. (See Chapter 15: Venture Capital Board) Because of their limited scope, whatever mistakes are made would not be a major threat to the central system nor to the overall economy.

20. *Banking crises will not be as detrimental to the overall economy and other financial systems* because these crises will not be as large or as influential in the monetary specter. Consequently, human hardships will be greatly reduced.

21. In actuality, the current disciplinary system (high interest rates), punishes the weakest, smallest players first and most severely, while the largest and more powerful enterprises are able to dodge the bullet. *The disciplinary systems of the current central banks protect the wealthy and punish the weak or not so wealthy —* because businesses and individuals on the lower end of the spectrum can't withstand high interest rates or lack of capital for operations.

Lack of diversification favors the wealthy and draws attention to one of the major flaws of capitalism — the rich get richer and the poor get poorer — the natural flow of capital concentrating in the wealthy.

I believe I have listed here more than enough reasons to support a diversity of monetary delivery systems. I'm sure you can see that these reasons both overcome the negatives of operating many systems and validate the need to be implemented in national economies.

11 ADDITIONAL MONETARY EXPANSION

Over the years, there have been numerous attempts by the monetary powers to stimulate growth. Unfortunately, the approach used to introduce new money has been under diversified, with only one delivery system — banks — and one vehicle — debt. This sort of system can and has favored the elite and the "hot" industries and leads to overcapacity. It can also over-stimulate the demand side of the equation, thus creating excess consumption and inflation.

If new money is introduced properly, with a matching increase in capacity and supply, more people are employed and demand is stimulated. The result: increased profits, wages and tax revenues.

Diversified, non inflationary, and sustained monetary expansion is an absolute necessity for continued economic growth. The equation is quite simple. The more money currently and correctly infused, the more investment and consumption, which means more employment. The more employment, the more economic health and the betterment of more lives.

This velocity of circulation (turnover) creates more total tax revenues, even with lower marginal rates to adequately fund the fiscal system, thus overcoming the negatives of capitalism. (See Chapter 6) This creates macroeconomic well being and accomplishes the funding of more diversified human endeavors

not normally acceptable to total financing by
private capital.

The real estate-home arena provides a recent example where capital infusion has created economic
wealth. A system of attainable mortgages (FHA, GI
Loans, Fannie Mae, Ginnie Mae, Development
Financing, etc.) has made the dream of owning a
home a reality for millions of families. In the process,
the industry is expanded, thereby creating many jobs.

For instance, California was fueled by this real estate
financing (monetary) and a military-aerospace infusion (fiscal). The result is that California has become
one of the economic giants of the world. This is a perfect illustration of how the introduction of capital can
increase employment, bolster industry and advance
civilization.

Even in natural disasters, we have seen the use of
SBA loans (monetary) and FEMA grants (fiscal) for
relief, which has slowed recession in the affected
areas, brought in growth and employment and
upgraded the communities.

Frankly, even *inefficient* capital infusion through deficit
spending distributes funds throughout the economic
regions of the country, providing benefits and jobs.

One of the major reasons capitalism has not spread
rapidly throughout the world, and has not succeeded
in feeding and housing a majority of the world's population, is the lack of efficient new money injection
and monetary supply. *Private capital and one central
banking system cannot do it alone!* The U.S. and other
developed nations have an easier time because of

their diversified financial services industry (old money) and well developed fiscal recirculation systems. It is much more difficult for Third World and old Communist countries for they rely mainly on one commercial banking system.

The *only* problem with creating funds and infusing them into the economy is excess inflation. The next chapter will address this problem.

Many economists believe that monetary policy is not the place to assist and stimulate growth. They believe this scenario cannot be effectively measured, monitored or enforced because of the long and unpredictable delays between changes in interest rates and their subsequent effects on the economy. They also believe that it is impossible through easier monetary policy to run the economy at a permanently high level of activity and/or lower rate of unemployment. These experts claim that inflating an economy only has a short run effect and everything will rise to maintain the same environment. Of course, this is true — if money is just increased with no controls or simply printed. These misguided beliefs continue to hinder our evolution into the next level of capitalism.

The questions become: How do we do it?, Where should it go?, Who should get it? and How should it be used? Should it be used to increase capacity and supply or to help consumers purchase more goods and services? What these economists never discuss is how to efficiently increase the monetary base and how to improve distribution.

They all discuss quantity, not quality. The quality depends on which individuals and firms new money is going to, what industries, and geographic regions. **This does not mean more government controls.** I'm suggesting the same type of arrangement as with the current banking system, which in essence, is licensed and controlled by government. I'm just recommending more than one delivery system.

Our global economy needs additional capital. Expansion of this capital, if put to productive use *cannot and will not create excessive inflation.*

If we eliminate monetary growth to zero, for an extended period we will have no growth and a depression. Therefore, monetary policy (new money) is needed to stimulate and increase commerce.

The current monetary system expands the monetary base willy nilly. It funds only successful overcapacity industries and companies, it sends money overseas and makes consumer debt too easy to attain. It is used for financial speculation to over-inflate assets such as property or stock. It can also be used to finance corporate mergers and acquisitions. Or it simply monetarizes the national debt. These functions are appropriate to a point, but the procedure is just not diversified enough.

Additional growth of the money supply should always be increasing and be geared to the needs of a growing population. New money is contract with the future, not a pure obligation to the past.

Besides excess inflation, the only other possible flaw in an expansive monetary policy is over-concentration in one industry (large or small, local or national). This is minor compared to excess inflation. Usually private business decisions limit this type of over-expansion, the result of which is a decline in prices, profits and bankruptcies. We see this in agriculture in the over-production of crops, and with real estate over-building. An effective diversified monetary system will also reduce the chances of this occurring in the economic environment. (See Chapter 6 — Flaws of Capitalization)

Under our current system there is limited control regarding new money (debt) for consumption (demand) as opposed to production (capacity). A more direct control of the additional increases in monetary supply can reduce the availability of capital for consumption, but not production, thus relaxing inflationary pressures on the current output of goods and services (capacity). Of course, overcapacity without demand results in recession-depression. The two big investment-led recoveries this century — America's in the 1920's and Japan's in the late 1980's ended in deep recession— depression.

My point is, **additional** monetary expansion can proceed *at a accelerated rate* when that money is used for the *production of a greater variety of services and goods* and when it is used for *finding natural resources*, rather than adding to consumer debt.

This is not to say that I am an advocate of supply-side economics. I am much more an advocate of demand-side economics (Keynesian), but I am a firm believer in supply-side monetary policy *when the monetary system encourages* **additional** *expansion*. Keynesian economics stresses the supposed benefits of having government manipulate aggregate demand, while supply-side economics stresses what the marketplace can produce.

E=mC^f

Expansion brings products and services to the market and employs labor (demand) to help consume that increase in products and services.

In short, I believe in demand-pushed economic expansion with the infusion of new money for its implementation. But all this has to be tempered so as to not exceed capacity, whereas producing new money unrelated to the diversified production of goods and services only creates excessive inflation.

In the past, excess capacity (supply) resulted in layoffs because of unmatched demand. This is the result of one of the major flaws in microeconomic vs. macro-economic capitalism. (see Chapter 6). But with adequate credit on the aggregate demand (money supply), fiscal recirculation, commensurate labor relations, and diversity in monetary distribution, oversupply of goods and services should not happen. This will solve the problems of excess capacity. The next chapter discusses the other side of the problem: excess inflation.

12 ELIMINATION OF EXCESS INFLATION

As I said, the only negative of an expansive monetary system is excess inflation. Having only one negative in a human institution makes it much easier to control. The following lists ways the monetary supply can be expanded without resultant excess inflation.

1) **Have more than one basic entity and more than one policy for dispensing the monetary supply.** This, in itself, aids in this diversity, relieving inflationary pressures. It increases the number of individuals and their enterprises which fuels competition and consequently keeps prices in check. The systems delivering the monetary supply should be varied geographically and more important, by industry, so that the supply of natural resources and other economic goods and services are not pressured by a high demand. It reduces inflation by increasing its dispersal.

2) **Direct the <u>additional</u> monetary supply towards increasing the output of a variety of goods and services (production) rather than consumption.** The more goods and services, the greater the competition, the less inflationary pressure. In other words, the excess increase in new money is strictly for domestic private enterprise which produces goods and services, including exploration, research, and development of natural resources. No goods and services are produced by many of the current loans, such as international and consumer loans, mortgage refinancing, and loans for mergers and acquisitions.

In fact, these loans can increase consumer spending, thus influencing inflation.

3) Implement other controls to insure that the interest rate is not the main regulator of the monetary supply. Interest rate hikes hit certain sectors harder than others, for example the residential industry. Use equity as well as debt to increase the monetary supply. Have different interest rate controls for different industries — such as residential real estate. Interest rates will do what the market for capital demands. It will continue to be a control on excess inflation by limiting the amount of new money demanded. The usual rise in interest rates have punished governments who issue too much inappropriate money. Higher interest rates will always continue to have some control on inflation.

4) Keep the number of bankruptcies low and enforce the collection of certain monetary programs. Well functioning economies need well designed bankruptcy procedures.

5) Encourage individuals and families to increase the private capital base, for example, by saving and investing for retirement. Just because there is an excess of new money does not mean there will be a direct pressure on the prices of consumer goods and services.

6) Encourage efficient monetary expansion, which leads to growth. This velocity of circulation eventually eliminates the fiscal deficit by generating more tax revenues. Keep in mind, where the national debt is monetarized, the fiscal deficit is a prime cause of inflation.

7) **Let the international currency markets aid in tracking excess inflation.** This will allow the monetary system to adjust to excess monetary creation. Traditionally, there have been two types of exchange rates: fixed and floating. I believe the record shows that fluctuating rates have worked better than fixed. Also we are far from having efficient currency markets. But this newer global market place is getting better and it will, and has, definitely punished nations that issue too much new money without effective economic commerce behind it.

Many consider the current crisis to be caused by capital flight from countries because of lack of capital controls. This outflow is usually a symptom — not a cause — of an inadequate monetary system or other severe economic problems.

8) **Expand the various statistical formulas (CPI, etc.) for measuring and predicting inflation.** Even if there is a difference of agreement on which formula is most appropriate, by using a number of formulae for evaluation — especially in the computer age — excess inflation can be measured in a range, which should enable it to be kept in check. Inflation measurements should be broad-based and include stocks, bonds and property as well as goods and services. This will help to control any asset or consumer bubble caused by over issuance of new money in any given area.

9) **Create a currency reserve system broader than gold. On the surface, this is seemingly an accounting function, but it does redirect responsibility and accountability.** The reserve could include other metals, energy reserves, government land, collateral or debt (mortgages) and non voting equity (See Chapter

14) and other government assets. This reserve would probably provide more of a psychological factor than a real reserve, but it would definitely help in currency stability between countries.

Currently the U.S. internal price inflation has been relatively low-to-moderate because the government is borrowing instead of printing (monetarization). This has extensively affected our currency exchange (external inflation). We've been lucky. Considering that the deficit has been used to fund non-production — social programs and military — internal inflation has been relatively calm.

The bottom line is this: my scenario of **an efficient — quality — and gradual monetary supply expansion is realistic and will not produce excess inflation.**

<u>13</u> DEBT AND EQUITY

When new money is singularly tied to the interest cycle, in an era of high rates, such as the early 1980's, the rich receive the greatest benefits and the poorer businessman is left holding the bag. The strongest are helped most by the government and many of the weakest are helped not at all. The disadvantaged continued to borrow just to stay in business. But high interest loans are only feasibly paid back when the economy continues to gallop out of control, when interest rates continue to escalate. Debts are subtly extinguished though price inflation, ameliorating the burden of the borrowers by depreciating the value of the dollars they must pay back. But in a singular system, such as we have now, when the economy settles down and rates drop, the low end businessman still has his high interest loans to pay back.

Of course there is another scenario. If the rates continue to climb higher, the power of compound interest takes over. It is such a strong and fundamental force in redistributing incomes, about the only relief is to break the impact of compound interest rates every so often, to write off the debts — or people are buried under a mountain of debt.

Historically, a recession or an economic collapse could evaporate that write-off. Debtors failed totally and debts were liquidated. Many got to start over again.

Where is it written that new money is created only through debt (loans)? By the way we cling to our old, antiquated system, you would think using debt to create money was one of the ten commandments.

This is silly. There is no reason why we can't establish institutions to partially fund new money through equity (common stock) structures, or a combination of debt and equity.

There is precedence for this. Believe it or not, Middle East (Islamic) banking provides equity return rather than just interest return. Because of religious beliefs, a mutual risk and a goal of non-clashing interests has developed into a shared risk banking. There is less adversarial relationship between lenders and borrowers.

Many things happen when there is no debt service. Business survival is heightened, competition increases, production is improved, consequently prices are kept down. There is less displacement of employers and employees. Even when interest rates rise, industries will continue to grow. The housing industry, usually the first hit by increasing interest rates, will stay healthy. If mortgage rates are lower, more folks can get into housing and sustain themselves. We are already seeing this in many fiscal programs of Federal and local governments. When business survival is heightened, there are fewer defaults in the banking system, which causes less strain on the entire financial system.

Any equity-new money system still yields return — and maybe even greater return — but it occurs upon sale or refinancing.

Internationally, especially in emerging markets, a diminished debt service would allow immature capitalistic enterprises to survive longer and mature into thriving enterprises. It would give the less advantaged an easier entry into today's capitalistic environment and a better chance for survival.

Of course, caution would have to be exercised here, so as to not give too much of advantage over competition financed through pure debt.

The raising of interest rates to control excess inflation will be burdensome to the survival of fewer people and their industries.

Besides the negative effects of high interest rates causing economic hardships, there are negatives to low interest rates. They offer less return to savers (i.e. retirees) who then spend less. The monetary system can over-expand too quickly causing excess inflation.

Also, the monetary system can help us out of a deep recession or depression — unlike the U.S. in the '30's and Japan in the '90's — through the use of equity. Commerce is not ready to borrow during a substantial decline — even if interest rates are at 1% or less because the climate is too severe. But enterprisers will be more willing to accept equity assurance, which does not have to be tied to debt service and is repaid only upon success!

Even fiscal expenditures can be funded using equity instead of tax dollars. For example, the government can fund a purchase by receiving stock or stock options. The success of the venture will bring value to the options, returning funds back to the government. Since there is a return, it can be funded by new money. (See Chapter 15, no. 13)

In an effective monetary creation program, in order to reduce the extreme negative effects of interest rates and the reluctance of private enterprise to invest, equity structures become an absolute necessity.

E=mC^f

<u>14</u> IMPLEMENTATION: THE FOURTH BRANCH OF GOVERNMENT

My recommendation for a dialogue to create an efficient, diversified, non-excessive inflationary monetary system should *not* be hindered by the discussion of who will have the power to operate it. **Implementation is much more important than the process of that implementation.**

In fact, in the first 125 years of our country, the main economic debates were centered around who was going to run the monetary system. The point is this: no matter what system or institution operates it, it will have the same human problems of power politics and there will be occasional errors in decision-making. The only way to reduce the impact of these glitches is to create diversity within these systems.

This book does not debate whether the monetary function should be established and regulated by government or private enterprise. **It is my opinion that it has to be established and regulated by some form of government oversight. It does not matter what system we use, whether it is some form of central, free, private or laissez-faire banking, currency boards or direct operation by the Treasury. The question should be: *how* will it be implemented?** In fact, the debate regarding who will operate the current monetary system and how it will function, has hidden the real solution for the wide-spread global monetary problem.

Accountability has been a very dicey political issue. But it is not the key to successful monetary disbursement and management.

As with the fiscal system, we will always have problems governing the monetary system. But with the current narrow and undiversified delivery, we cannot solve these problems, only accentuate them when error occurs. No matter how good the controlling entity is at handling the current monetary system, because of the flaws in the system, it will still have the same old snafus.

Our present political setup is too immature to adequately operate a monetary system, much less to initiate the changes necessary to correct the failings of monetary delivery systems. Let's face it, in our current stage of political development, there is just too much pork in the barrel. Special interests prohibit political effectiveness.

Control should initially continue through an independent entity like the current Federal Reserve Board and the central banks around the world. Control is not the key issue. Any changes of control structure will be made by legislators after rigorous debate.

Let me be crystal clear here: *a huge governmental bureaucracy does not need to be created for this purpose.* I am simply recommending that there be numerous banking systems to infuse new money into the system. In fact, I think **implementation should probably**

remain with the Federal Reserve (the Central Banks) for the near future — with possibly a series of sub-boards running each new monetary delivery system and the central board overseeing and strictly controlling the amount allocated to each. Where else can we find a storehouse of trained economists and operators of monetary systems? I repeat, eliminating central banking control is not the answer!

Any system with this much power must be controlled and disciplined by an inner profession. Like any system, there will be errors, adjustments and illegal activities. This is true in any human endeavor. Therefore, the monetary system must have *checks and balances* to minimize criminal activity, prevent excessive monetarization, keep bankruptcies at a minimum, and enforce collections.

Especially since most of these monetary systems will partner with private enterprise, I picture a very small bureaucracy to oversee them. Also, the operational budget would be rather small, so it should be funded by the monetary side, not the fiscal side, with a monetary inspector general to enforce compliance. The reality is that creating money is a very profitable activity. If you have a monopoly on its creation and you can keep some of the profits, it can easily pay for itself.

Whenever new systems are implemented, they must be done GRADUALLY. We are not recommending immediate and massive increases in the monetary supply. Sudden shocks to any system can have adverse economic consequences.

Over the years and around the globe, our central banks have been involved in various types of operations, under the guise of many titles. They have been widely criticized for the ways they conducted business. This is the way of the human being. *No matter how educated we are, no matter how advanced our mathematical formulas, our activities will never be perfect.*

This book is not a critique of these operations and who controls them. (There are many books that do just that!) No matter what organization sits atop the pyramid controlling the money supply, only a diversified implemented system will reduce the effect of error. Improving the current delivery system (commercial banking) will always help — but it's not the answer!

I am not concerned with *who* runs the system but *how* it is delivered. Economists are legendary for not agreeing on anything. Therefore, I am simplifying my recommendations to six simple basic strategies. Specifics and implementation can be debated later.

SUMMARY OF CHANGES

1. *Institute many more systems to deliver new money.*

2. *Have an efficient, expansive, growth-oriented monetary policy.*

3. *Increase the motivation of more individuals and businesses to invest in these systems as a way to further increase the availability of new money.* In other words, increase the system's reserves.

4. *Use equity as well as debt to deliver new money.*

5. *Mainly worry about excess inflation* as the primary target — not interest rates, monetary supply or aggregates, growth rates, price stability, or other indicators.

6. *Use the <u>additional</u> expansion of new money for producing a greater amount and a greater variety of goods and services and for developing natural resources* (supply). Consequently, it can be increased at a much greater rate.

7. *Introduce a formal monetary structure to the people, and educate them on its use.* (See Chapters 16 and 17.)

15 CURRENT AND POTENTIAL NEW MONETARY DELIVERY SYSTEMS

As we've already discussed, fiscal power is delivered through many different systems. The Federal government has numerous agencies making decisions, in addition to local (state, county, city) governments which add substantial diversity in delivery.

At present, we have one commercial banking system dispersing a major economic governmental power. *It can and has been prone to major error.* Oversupply and over capacity hampers growth, it can over-expand industry, bear no relation to the production of goods and services and it discriminates against non-wealthy clients. **Oversupply and over capacity are prime causes of deep recession or depression.**

One of the Fed's favorite weapons, raising interest rates, is only sporadically effective as a hedge against inflation. Higher interest rates can cause debtors to borrow more and more to keep up with their old debts and interest payments. In fact, if they want to stay afloat, they have no choice. This process too often continues to bankruptcy buyout.

Humans make errors. Institutions run by humans exacerbate these errors and always will.

Having one single system can only compound the

problems when errors are made. Only a latticework of multiple delivery systems will reduce the significance of any errors — whether on the expansion or restriction side.

The world needs capital to fund, expand, explore, invent, research and to create goods and services. Private capital (old money) cannot do it alone. Unrelated to the fiscal side, the government has to take a role in capital formation. Unfortunately, their current monetary role operates in just one system, using debt only.

A monetary policy coordinated and delivered will be more *broad-based and less influenced by excessive need* and in tune with inflation factors (available natural resources, labor, infrastructure and competition). The end result is the production and consumption of goods and services with a potential return or collateral (debt and/or equity) for a federal government.

The following is a list of 15 different monetary systems that should be considered for the new monetary structure. Some are currently in operation, some are new and different. Each of them can provide either collateral or a rate of return back to the government besides taxation.

1. *Federal Reserve-Commercial Banks.* **The current commercial banking system should issue less new money.** The FRB can also control the dollar supply without using substantial interest rate fluctuations — resulting in more control of consumption and production allocation. **This proposal does not recommend dismantling the banking system nor does it suggest tampering with the current bond markets.**

Any system needs constant review and improvement. We can also explore the addition of an equity component to the current commercial banking system. But we still need additional systems.

Simply reduce the amount of new money that is allowed through the commercial banking system (less reliance on their reserve system) and give it to the institutions operating in other systems. This reduction is more important in many of the other nations of the world who have less control and less developed commercial banking systems. Then the IMF will have fewer bailout problems.

2. *A myriad of financial services and insurance firms* can provide banking services and money creation. In particular, the U.S. has a very well developed Financial Services industry. This industry can provide the delivery of new money through many of its current structures and financial vehicles.

For example, a mutual fund can be established that allows for a reasonable creation of new money, say, 10-30% on top of the contributions of its investors. Commercial banks use a 500-900% reserve factor. This money can support expansion by being placed in debt and equity in various industries. It need not be used for investment in already existing stock. Instead, the conditions could create new commerce like IPO's, plant-equipment expansion, research and development, etc.

Having a variety of non-banks as an additional source of new money distribution will create the geographical and industry diversity needed for an effective monetary delivery system. There have been several ideas floating around in this arena, such as equity banking, and other private banking concepts that can be explored.

Commercial banks are competing heavily in non bank services, such as insurance and investments, so non financial corporations and financial companies — profit and <u>non-profit</u> — should also be allowed systems of new money creation. Large securities firms, such as Merrill Lynch, Dean Witter, Paul Webber, etc. can be directly given some monetary creating power (with regulation). They now have to go through banks for new money — but they do provide a lot of other banking services now!

Liberalization of the Glass-Steagall Act is not what I'm talking about. This allows banks to move into other industries by acquiring these firms and non-banks to acquire banks. But the method of new money creation is still in the commercial banking delivery system.

3. *Federal Venture Capital Board.* A board can be created to provide new money to those industries and in those regions that need capital, instead of issuing these funds through debt, which has to be serviced. This board would invest new money through non-voting stock (equity). Meaning: *absolute, non-controlling silent equity.* This infusion can be helpful in any arena, such as natural resource exploration, manufacturing, service, housing, high tech, low tech. It can aid any region: state, county, or city. It can startup or aid any size enterprise, small, medium or large.

Instead of debt, the board will retain a *non-controlling, non-voting,* equity interest. (It would have to be non-voting — one doesn't want any hint of socialism.) Therefore, upon sale, liquidation, dividends or refinancing, the government would receive a return on its equity interest.

Like the current FRB, the operation of this board can be independent of Congress, ensuring non-political allocation decisions, at the same time becoming more needs-directed. The non-voting equity can be held as a reserve by the board, like the gold at Fort Knox. The non-voting stock can be managed similarly to any portfolio management with certain liquidity controls. If the stock is public, sales of this equity must be managed without substantial price fluctuations. Private equity would be held for sale or liquidation.

With all the brain power we have on Wall Street, I am sure we could create an appropriate management system.

This is **not** strictly a government-run operation. Similar to our current banking system, it should be a joint venture with venture capitalists and investment bankers.

This board can operate in three ways. First, it can provide capital to supplement current venture capitalists and investment bankers. For example, the board would give these already existing firms a 20%-50% increase in their available capital per project. None would be solely funded by the board. The board would simply supply a portion of all the investments of the participating investment banker.

Second, the board could create a whole new array of firms that would directly provide new equity capital for needed areas and deserving companies. They could coordinate with other sources of debt funding, i.e., commercial banks, SBA, FHA, to provide 100% of a funding source.

Third, the government could have its own internal allocation system that could fund direct equity grants to large and small firms in needy areas.

Examples: A Fortune 1000 company is considering a plant. If the company places it in an area of the country that needs employment, the venture capital board invests 10%-50% of the capital requirements for this plant. In return, the board receives non-voting equity, such as stock options. Management would certainly be attracted to not having to use its own capital and no interest payments, but if the fundable areas are undesirable for its operation, they wouldn't take the capital for the plant. The relationship should not be adversarial. Still, the low cost capital would be an incentive to move certain operations into depressed areas.

Another example allocates capital to new, small businesses in blight areas. If the owner is qualified, if the business is needed, the infusion of money would provide immediate employment and services to the region. The absence of interest payments enhances the survival rate of enterprises in these poorer areas. This is somewhat like the SBA, but with a return to the government through equity capital. Certainly, this is a higher risk scenario, but it also has higher returns. Most importantly, all the activities will provide for the exploration and production of goods and services that keep inflation in check. Capital is immediately put to work, resulting in more employees and the stimulation of the economy.

This non-voting equity could also be applied to real estate financing for needy families. (There are similar programs in existence, but they are limited in scope.) Many families with successful employment histories cannot come up with a down payment or afford 100% financing programs. This funding would provide down payments. A return to the government can come from sale or refinance. Otherwise, it remains an asset of the government.

This board would eliminate the trickle-down effect of our monetary system. It can provide capital without collateral for those entrepreneurs who present effective business plans and existing businesses who need additional capital (without sufficient collateral), and for areas of blight which need firms, both small and large to enter their areas.

The Federal Reserve Venture Capital Board represents a joint effort with private capital, mainly infused through private enterprise. The major distinction is the absence of debt service. The lack of a cash flow drain enhances the chances of success. Of course, there will be allocation errors, but not to the extent that the current banking system has made throughout its existence, mainly because this would be a more diverse and smaller total infusion. Increasing the variety of goods and services is extremely healthy for an economic environment.

I want to reiterate something here. Some people feel that the government is too heavily involved in my recommendations. This is not correct. Most of my recommendations are with separate licensing private organizations similar to our banking structure. Yes, a small amount can be delivered by a direct government agency, but it is not the essence of my doctrine.

4. *Community Banking System* — support the passage of new laws to provide capital to disadvantaged regions and deserving people. How about <u>adding a non-voting equity side</u> along with debt? (See Chapter 14). There is already a separate banking system established in the less wealthy regions of our country. This system can be used to expand the money supply into enterprise areas such as inner city ghettos. Nonetheless, it shouldn't be limited to inner city enterprises. It should be used to expand the business, real estate and consumer loan market. Equity financing is a must. Survival in a lower economic area needs help, by reducing the debt servicing costs (interest expense). This does not mean that completely unqualified borrowers are funded. All loan debt and equity should meet specified tests of management quality and ability — but not necessarily be confined to collateral.

An example of this is **"micro-credit."** In less developed parts of the world, peasants are lifting their families — and even entire villages — out of poverty after receiving loans of $20 or less to start their own businesses. The idea that the poor can be just as enterprising as anyone else if given access to credit — no matter how small — led to the creation of the Grameen Bank in Bangladesh. This idea is just catching on in the U.S.

5. *Additional local profit and non-profit bank-like entities* — not strictly located in New York's Wall Street or the commercial banking system — *can be created to meet demands for more capital.*

6. Current *real estate financing mortgages* (Fannie Mae, Ginnie Mae, Freddie Mae, etc.) could provide non-

voting equity capital (non debt) to needy families so they can own their own homes. Similar funding already exists throughout the country. It should be greatly expanded, assuming we have the production capability. This monetary expansion — starting with the GI loans after World War II — is an excellent example of my theory. The next level of capitalism builds on this success.

Additionally, the current low income housing programs provides another prime example. The joint efforts of the Federal government, private enterprise and the commercial banking system is solving a dire need.

7. *Small Business Administration* — should be expanded not contracted, with a rate of return back to the Federal government for guaranteeing loans. Equity as well as debt financing should also be used for already mentioned reasons. This program should be both expanded and localized not just federally, but also on the state, county and city levels.

8. *Student Loan System* — should be expanded at very reasonable terms with enforced collection. The current system provides a return to the Treasury, but the Bureaucracy is managing it. The Student Loan system should be operated by private enterprise with a benefit back to the Treasury. Most important: A college education should not be a matter of money! Student loan rates should be set at below-market costs, with long term maturities and fixed-low rates. These rates should be high enough to simply cover defaults and some administration.

9. Research & Development System *R & D Board* — needs a return potential or it should be transferred to

the fiscal side. On the monetary side, an enhanced research and development system would disperse funds to educational and private business institutions for projects that have potential return from royalties, patents or other salable potential. If these returns are nebulous or hard to attain, they should be funded on the fiscal side where no return is expected. This type of monetary system would be quite small in actual implementation but it would provide additional diversity for the issuance of new money.

10. *Federal State & Municipal Loan System* — An additional system can be created along with the municipal bond industry to help governments (state, county, city) fund various local projects. The returns would come from ongoing interest payments or end-point payout (like zero coupons). New money factors would be added to the municipal bond underwriting — say at a 10-20% level. (The Fed does this somewhat now in their direct loans of non-marketable debt.)

11. *Bailouts* — Institute a monetary system for corporate and real estate bailouts — the type of system that could have resolved a Chrysler situation or Resolution Trust (Savings and Loan/Real Estate). This system would retain a percentage of equity so that there would be a long range return to the government. If Chrysler and the RTC had a small (10%-20%) equity position in these bailouts, it would have more than paid for itself.

12. *Foreign Country Systems* — International systems such as the (IMF) International Monetary Board, (WB) World Bank and Commercial Bank Loans for international lending already exist. They are having many problems because they are part of a single sys-

tem issuing debt only. Wherever international finance is backed by a Federal government, a return should be provided to that government.

13. Create an *Infrastructure Board* for upgrading and retooling roads, bridges, water, dams and the like — such as the current ATP — but emanating from the monetary side with some being a joint venture with private capital.

14. *Government contracts* — When a government issues contracts to the private sector, such as for the purchase of military hardware, it is always financed by the fiscal side. It can also be partially financed by the monetary side, through loans and equity participation. Say, for example, a private aerospace firm receives a multi billion dollar contract. Initially, it is funded with tax dollars but in return the government could receive stock options for awarding the contract. Of course, this would be on a limited basis because of dilution and market ability. Then, when the options are exercised, capital would be returned back to the government, replacing pure tax funding. Again, this creates diversity.

15. *Conservation Board* — setup to create money for purchase of additional public lands (parks) for environmental and recreational purposes. This land is a non-wasting asset. It would be held as collateral (reserves), offsetting inflationary concerns. Purchase of various land parcels that schools and other projects sit on can be an effective disbursement of new money. When the land is not used for that purchase, the land could be resold, and the proceeds returned to the government. Consequently, the land would be collateral for additional diversity expansion of the monetary supply.

16. *New information age* (Cybermoney) — Banking and financial instruments are entering the computer age. There has already been a development in monetary-creation. It is called E-money — new global money created without national boundaries and central banks. Will it work? Who will control it? The answers aren't clear at this time, but whatever the future brings, this new money will provide a diversification factor and change our monetary systems.

Certainly, cybermoney — in all its divergent forms — has developed into something of a controversial issue. Simply speaking, there are two kinds of electronic money: 1) smart (or prepaid) cards, where a given amount is stored on a plastic card; and 2) digital cash (internet money) wherein the medium is the computer hard disk.

Smart cards are good for limited amounts of cash and of all the various innovations in payment transactions, "smart" cards have gotten the most buzz. But smart cards don't present the biggest challenges to a stubborn banking system and its singular monetary policy. Digital cash — still an ongoing experiment with a huge growth prediction — is best used for long-distance payments and its effect on the system is just getting noticed. The operable point is this: *digital cash supplants book money* and could possibly be a thorn in the side of monetary policy.

Follow this progression: 1) Digital cash takes payments off the banks' books, so demand for central-bank money — a cornerstone of monetary policy — is reduced. 2) The role of cash declines. 3) If internet lending does not require minimum reserves, the scope for credit creation expands. 4) The velocity (circulation of money) increases because transactions can be handled more quickly on the internet. 5) Monetary growth diminishes as an accurate barometer of inflationary potential (smart cards are included in the monetary aggregates, digital cash is not) 6) Digital cash will also be used for international payments (the internet is a country without borders). Effectively, this means that volumes of transfers not recorded by normal domestic money supply data will be influencing the demand for goods and services.

Assuming no new, comprehensive international regulations, the volume generated by digital money will dwarf smart cards. We will be up to our necks in monetary policy problems. The solution — adequately integrating cybermoney into the existing accounting system — has already begun. Germany has enacted legislation that explicitly defines digital money transfers as banking business, with necessary cover reserves. And, even though it will be challenging, central banks the world over must band together to overcome the impact that digital payments have on monetary policy.

There are many systems that can be created to provide a diversified infusion of new money. **Most of these systems depend on a partnership of public and private capital, but are implemented by private enterprise.** This results in more commerce, bringing in more tax revenue, which makes it much easier to balance the fiscal budget — even with lower marginal rates. The government can also require compliance with basic laws, i.e. minimum wages, environmental, health care, safety.

So, these are just a few of the concepts that can be created to diversify the new monetary supply. Obviously, some would be greater than others and operations of these institutions would have to be intelligently established, but it's a start and other ideas will certainly spring from this beginning.

This book doesn't discuss exact operations or techniques for measurement for each delivery system, nor does it comprehensively focus on the how-tos of an entire monetary re-structure. This will come later, with multiple input from economic specialists and business leaders, through political discussion, serious research and healthy debate.

16 RESTRUCTURE THE ECONOMICS OF FEDERAL GOVERNMENTS

Federal Governments should be managed by two operational budgets, one monetary, the other fiscal. With a diversified and expansive monetary budget, the fiscal budget should easily be balanced.

The point I've been making throughout is that the monetary side of government should be in charge of creating money for efficient infusion into the economy. **In my plan, the monetary side will always be collateralized, meaning a rate of return will accrue back to the government (either interest, profit or some sort of collateral in a non-wasting asset).** Since governments are basically not profit making enterprises, there is no time requirement for this return, nor a specific need for the amount of return. Only excess inflation matters. Limited losses are just dissolved within the inflation rate. Governments don't have to report to owners or a stock market. **And the fiscal side will still provide the programs that do not bring a return or collateral and are paid by taxes.**

To implement this, the first major change would be to place all the governmental capital delivery systems that bring a return on investment into the monetary side. This would include the SBA, Community Bank, RTC, IMF, college loans, low income housing, corporate bailouts, and some newer monetary delivery systems (See chapter 15) along with the various real estate lending systems. Some of these functions do not currently yield a return to government, but that can be easily installed with debt and/or equity. More than likely, several other programs such as research and development, can be transferred to the monetary side, as long as government adds a return potential. Also, the so called "off book guaranteed" items can be transferred to the monetary side, initiating a return back to the government for providing these guarantees. The cost of new money is basically nothing. Currently the profits of this operation go to the fiscal side of government. It should be that these profits are used first to pay off any national debt.

The fiscal budget is a future plan for how much you are going to spend and receive. The actual amounts are what count. If you have an real deficit, the government needs to borrow funds. If it is an actual surplus — shouldn't it go to pay off any debt?

Then the budgetary process doesn't have to be that fine-tuned. Legislators can be more concerned with specific programs and simpler tax regulations — especially, if the monetary system helps fund some of the expenses. (Social Security funding is a separate discussion which I will not tackle in this book.)

Let us set up a balance sheet depicting the government's assets along with its debt. Government can list the market values of assets acquired by fiscal spending (capital budget) for investments like roads or purchase of land (infrastructure), then with a restructured monetary system, list the government's loans and equities as assets.

On the income statement, let the government start operating on a more business-like basis by increasing non-tax revenues such as leasing rights, royalties from grants, printing, tariffs and payments for its services to other countries. Then with the restructured monetary system, return on loans and equities can be listed as income.

Admittedly, this type of accounting is probably best suited for politics and the psychology of the population. Emotions play a very important role in economics.

This restructure presents a clearer picture of the economic makeup of Federal governments. *This will help the population understand its government better and lower their anxiety; an anxiety that can cause the citizenry to view a Federal government as a business or household, which it is not! Individuals and businesses do not have the power to create new money!* Our 19th Century classical (industrial age) view of economics does not meet the diverse capital needs of the 21st century. This has been proven time and time again.

Having governments create new money through multiple systems (organizations), most in partnership with private capital and implemented through private enterprise, will result in more commerce and increased wages. This brings in greater tax revenue, making it easier to balance the budget even with reduced tax brackets.

The current deficit is mainly controlled by our government's fiscal policy. Nonetheless, there is a substantial portion of the budget that is controlled by the monetary side. In actual fact, our congressional branch has limited power in controlling the interest rate on the national debt. Interest rates have fluctuated between 2% and 20% in the last few decades. It makes it more difficult for Congress to balance the budget when the FRB-Treasury-marketplace controls this expense.

When the FRB attempts to reduce inflation, it raises interest rates, which eventually slows growth and employment. This in turn increases unemployment benefits, decreases tax revenues and adds interest expense on the deficit, resulting in an even larger deficit. Common sense seems to be absent from this scenario. Also, the FRB can raise interest rates for other economic reasons, which causes the budget to be unbalanced again. Errors in the monetary (banking) system, like the savings and loan collapse, force the fiscal side to repay depositors with fiscal side spending — again widening the deficit.

When a central monetary system attempts to reduce inflation or perceived inflation in the future, it generally has certain tools to implement this counter-inflationary environment. It can raise interest rates and increase the reserves requirement at the commercial banks. This slows lending which slows monetary growth (expansion of new money into the system).

This reduction causes commerce to decelerate, thereby producing less jobs, taxes and employment. With decreased employment, society receives more governmental spending in social benefits (unemployment insurance, welfare, etc.). With less jobs and commerce, there is less tax money to go around, thereby increasing the deficit. Consequently, higher interest rates cause the Treasury to increase its interest costs on the national debt...bringing about a greater deficit.

Up to now, the Federal government has provided capital and benefits through its monetary and fiscal policies. It mainly receives a return through taxation. There is some return from the Federal Reserves out of profits. Yet, *we are always trying to cut taxation!* Having a healthier return in non-tax revenue on the monetary side of government would offset fiscal expense and bring enormous benefits. Among them, currency stability, population psychology, reduced deficit and less taxation pressure.

Again, I have not gone into exact detail as to how this new structure will be implemented, operated or measured. There will be many ways to accomplish the same objectives. This is up to future leaders and economists.

<u>17</u> EDUCATE THE PUBLIC

"War is much too serious a matter
to be entrusted to the military.
Money creation is much too serious a matter
to be enshrouded in secrecy."

M odern Americans, educated in the conceit of
ever-upward progress and comfortable with
complex technologies unimagined a hundred years
ago, assume that in every way they are more sophisticated and knowledgeable than their forebears from
the last century. Mostly this is true, but the politics
and understanding of money is an important exception. Citizens of the nineteenth century were routinely familiar with the political implications of
monetary policy and debated the question fiercely
among themselves even on the homesteads in the
"Wild West".

Unencumbered by the cryptic nature of modern economics, ordinary people formed their own opinions
on complicated aspects of money and credit, topics
that in the 20th Century have become reserved for
experts and technocrats only.

This has to cease, and one of the objectives of this
book is to start the discussions again! If capitalism is to
grow into a successful world order in the 21st Century,
we must lift the veil and reeducate ourselves.

In a democracy, we can't rely on public servants to
do our thinking for us. They can help us contem-

plate the potential consequences of various choices, but we, the indefatigable public, must make these choices for ourselves. At the same time, the poll takers love to tell us what the public really wants. This modern day obsession with polls can be disastrous for a democracy. Point in fact, the public doesn't ever know what it wants until its had the chance to discuss, debate and deliberate.

It's the duty of our political leaders to educate, to persuade, to dialogue with the public. Democracy demands disclosure, deliberation, discussion and discovery. Our citizenry has become lazy. If we're going to have the Millennium we dream of, we need to take responsibility for our lives and become engaged in the process.

WHAT DO YOU KNOW ABOUT THE FED?

The news media treats the Fed like a protectorate. The public seldom hears what the Federal Reserve governors have to say because the media doesn't bother to report it. Unarguably, the Federal Reserve is the center post of the American system. With a keystroke, decisions by the Fed alter the lives and fortunes of millions — if not billions — of mostly unaware citizens. Yet, the press treats these decisions as though they were of interest only to a few bankers, economists and Wall Street denizens. If John Q. Public does cultivate interest in the activities of the Fed, he must search out the financial section and wade through obscure jargon that only financial mukiwuks can read.

More alarming, the press tends to treat the workings of the central bank like a kindly grandfather who sits above the fray, never makes mistakes and is somehow detached from the messy goings on in the DC combat zone.

From all reports, our Federal Reserve governors are essentially removed from the uglier ramifications of their official deliberations. They focus exclusively on the complex technical issues of money hydraulics. The impact that these dollar decisions have on the store clerk, the traveling salesman and the factory worker is <u>not</u> part of their mandate. Equity or inequity, satisfaction or suffering is not their concern.

What very few people outside the circle know is how powerful one clique is in forging its will on the Fed. This almighty interest group includes the bankers, the bondholders, the brokers and their investors. They watch the Fed like a mother hen, demanding that their agendas be paramount. Naturally, these interests are narrow-casted and flagrantly self serving and directly affect the lives of every single American. In the present system, no citizen sits outside the shadow of the Federal Reserve. Moreover, it will stay that way until someone is brave enough to mount a challenge.

THE LESSON OF HISTORY

If we're willing, we can learn from history. Our experience of the last 25 years shows us that trying to control credit by interest rates alone is folly — fundamentally ineffective and inequitable. The strong get stronger, the weak get weaker. The borrowers are punished while the lenders are rewarded. The free market is absolute fiction

Additionally, we learn that the politicos are all-but-committed to the status quo. The political elite — elected officials, economic experts, the media — historically cling to conventional wisdom and acceptable political thinking.

Here's the painful part: if we read our history, we find that actual transformation of economic belief just doesn't happen until there is a great, recognizable disaster, such as the collapse of 1929. The painful result of a crash like this disgraces conventional wisdom and opens the door for fresh ideas. Economists — defenders to the end of the status quo — are always the last to know when old structures are falling and new ones taking their place. In Populist time, they ridiculed the agrarian reformers who saw the flaws of the gold system. During the Great Depression, they blasted all ideas of an expansive fiscal policy. The next batch of economists adopted Keynesian orthodoxy only to be dealt a lethal dose of stark reality.

I want to change this scenario. Politicians and economists (and by proxy, the general public) tend to close the barn door after the horse is gone. I want this book to lead the way to a new economic paradigm, and in so doing to forestall crisis, both home and abroad. Financial stability demands greater and quicker disclosure of information from banks, governments, companies and international institutions everywhere.

In the U.S. right now, we're going through good times and let's face it, it's much more difficult to improve things when we're not in crisis. This is the reason I'm bringing this book out now. With the proper will, we can gradually change and overcome our mistakes of implementation when we're not in economic upheaval. It takes bold leadership to develop and improve our systems at times like this. In truth, I expect monetary restructuring to be implemented first in countries that are having problems.

What is also important is to start educating our children at young ages in personal finance and basic economics. It is amazing to me that a country that embraces capitalism and self reliance has such limited education in these important areas.

CONCLUSION

Writing this book has been a labor of love. I've thought about the incongruencies and complexities in the current economic structure for most of my adult life. What has inspired me to put these thoughts on paper and share them with you, has little to do with theory and philosophy. Without the human element, economics is as dry a science as mathematics. When economists debate the vagaries of one economic structure versus another, too little emphasis is put on the contributions to society that these structures would produce.

This is not a pure research book. I wanted to make it as short as possible, enabling more readership to help me induce change. Therefore, I have not footnoted or given credit to other writers or economists, nor have I tried to prove every statement or concept I have used.

<u>VISION</u>

In my vision, the adjustments to our economic system — as outlined in this book — would greatly enhance and accelerate the quality of life on our planet. Ultimately, that's the point and purpose of $E=mC^f$.

I envision that all people on earth have *enough to eat*, are *reasonably housed*, have *sufficient work* and adequate *health care*. 21st Century capitalism will have no have nots, only those that have more.

I envision the *elimination of our ghettos* by a massive infusion of capital, both old and new, through a diversified monetary system and an efficient fiscal system; lower income participants, wealthy individuals and corporate enterprises would equally contribute.

I envision the local *financial burden of education being reduced* by a new monetary system that purchases land for school buildings, holds it as collateral, and when not needed for educational purposes, receives a return upon sale. Therefore, local fiscal systems have more money to spend on teachers, supplies, buildings and even funding pre-school education.

I envision *third world economies being more quickly moved out of the dark economic ages and into modern capitalism*; the customer bases of these countries are better established through diversified monetary and fiscal systems that more efficiently recirculate money.

I envision *cancer and many other diseases being cured over the next several decades* because of the increased expenditures of an efficient fiscal system, a diversified monetary system and favorable private enterprise.

I envision the *space budget tripling* because of increased revenues from an efficient monetary system, enhancing velocity of circulation while lowering tax rates; consequently employing more college graduates in the *exploration and colonization of our solar system*.

I envision that the sovereign nations of the world will stand together and *prioritize our planet's ecology*. We the people will truly begin to respect and appreciate mother earth — the source of our existence. We will replenish her rain forests, heal the O zone and eliminate pollution as a life-threatening force.

I envision the *oceanography budget quintupling;* thereby employing more college graduates in the *exploration, farming and preservation of our oceans.*

I envision that *all careers and occupations will have a place in the future.* We are flying at the speed of light through the information age. As the economic world gets more efficient and productive, especially through the use of the Internet, we will need less and less employees to produce all the goods and services we need for comfortable lives. $E=mCf.$ will allow many more to explore expanded careers in the arts, music, research, the sciences, etc.

E=mC^f

THE ERROR OF ALL OTHER THEORIES

There are many macroeconomic theories, doctrines and philosophies. To jot down just a few: classical, neo classical, new classical, Keynesian, Keynesian Unemployment, New Keynesian, New Neo Keynesian, Monetarism and Supply Side. Trust me, there will be more out next week.

I don't have time in this book to describe and counter each of these philosophies nor do you want me to wade through this dialogue. Here's what you need to remember: **none of them is comprehensive enough to create a quality 21st Century economic environment for all of us.**

You see, **these doctrines have at least one thing in common: they have all failed to consider how new money is allocated within their monetary policy.** Their debate is centered around the quantity of money and not the quality. They assume that the single commercial banking and interest rate controlled structure of past and present is the only way to carry out the distribution of new money. They all fail to adequately comprehend the failure in our monetary systems to adequately distribute a diversity of new money to the economy. All these theories, doctrines, formulas and measurements assume that the banking systems distribute (new) money efficiently — meaning that they have the diversity to promote widespread commerce and prosperity without boom-bust scenarios.

In actual fact, a single system cannot do this and it *makes all macroeconomic-monetary doctrines, models and formulas invalid,* as proven by human economic history. Trying to improve and discuss our macroeconomic system by concentrating the debate on only fiscal policy is a fatal error and economically bankrupt.

Improving the risk models, regulations and operational methods of our central and commercial banks will help, but not solve this inherent delivery flaw. Because of human frailty and boom-bust scenarios (bubble economy), *lack of diversity will always lead to drastic financial shock and failure.*

Unfortunately, the discipline of economics fails to examine out of its own context. **The continuing efforts of economists to improve their delivery formulas only refers to the *quantity* of the monetary supply, with very little attention to the *quality*.** Quality depends on where it is going in terms of who (firms and individuals), what (industries), and where (regions).

This flaw is currently accentuated in international economies — financial enterprises not as diversified as the U.S. and other seasoned single-monetary systems.

Monetary systems have to improve internally in order to avoid problems from external capital funds. I did not want to tackle the international relationships between countries, their foreign reserves, trade balances, tariffs, capital flows and control, exchange rates, free trade issues, low cost-slave labor and the inter-relationships of their monetary systems. This is a topic for another time. Moreover, these inter-relationships get a little paradoxical and complicate my explanation to improve the systems around the world.

What you need to remember is this: **most countries of the world suffer in some way from the lack of**

diversity in their monetary systems. The U.S. and Europe suffer the least, and Asia and third world countries the most. The industrialized U.S. and Europe have mature, reasonably run central-commercial banking systems and very developed "old money" financial firms. The diversity of the monetary delivery systems in these countries will just take us to the next level of capitalism. In the third world and ex-Communist countries, they have neither effective banking or non-banking financial institutions and you can see the difference. (See Chapter 5). Therefore, it is more important in third world countries to have a diversified monetary system, so they can implement successful capitalism.

<u>PARADOXES — CATCH 22's</u>

The discipline of economics and its ancillary theories has its opposites and paradoxes. In other words, what any economist may say, for whatever purpose, usually can be countered with an opposite reasoning. Some of the following contradictions are related to monetary policy.

1. We have to *charge high credit risks a greater interest rate to make up for the extra losses.* But, of course, the higher rate makes it harder for the least able to pay their loans back. The result: more defaults, bankruptcies and human suffering.

2. *Higher interest rates (or restricting credit) to reduce the monetary supply.* At the same time they increase the cost of loans to business, which can lead to excess bankruptcies. This puts bad loans on the

lender books — resulting in banks going under — eventually bringing about crisis in the entire financial system.

3. If *inflation's bad, and deflation's bad...what's good?!*

4. It's sensible to *reduce human commerce and growth and increase human suffering because its leads to inflation.*

5. Competition is good, competition is god — so let's *increase competition until we have created a total oversupply and capacity, resulting in falling prices and bankruptcies* for all but the well endowed.

6. Government securities are financed partially by banks. All well and good, but *when there is a credit crunch, financial institutions cannot borrow enough government bonds — thereby creating a potential crisis.*

7. *When the economy needs more new money* (loans), instead of lending money, *banks buy government bonds* that provide no risk and a reasonable rate of return, thereby *reducing economic growth.*

8. *Higher interest rates cause a decrease in taxation from less economic activity and an increase in government social expenditures.* These factors then again widen the budget deficit in a never-ending cycle of economic structure.

9. Tax surpluses have only nominally been used to repay any major part of the national debt. *The larger the national debt, the larger the interest charge on that debt, therefore the larger the annual fiscal deficit.* This circular link has resulted in greater and greater national debt.

10. The fiscal side of government attempts to make up the slack for the current single, underdiversified monetary system with its programs and deficit spending. *Then, to cover its deficit spending, it mostly borrows money instead of creating it. Consequently, the interest rate factor compounds the deficit.*

⋙⋙

SUMMARY: GOALS OF THIS BOOK

The following summarizes the goals of this book which I want the national governments of the world to implement.

1. *Multiple delivery systems.* Our global monetary (new money) system needs a *multitude of delivery operations* to provide greater diversity, geographically, for individuals and for industry. Diversification brings more entrepreneurs and their enterprises into the capitalistic system. Adding a host of delivery systems would eliminate excess inflation, boom-bust scenarios, and produce a continuous, expandable high growth economic environment. The bottom line: more benefits to more people — quality, not just quantity.

2. *Equity.* Equity, as well as debt, should be used for the issuance of new money. This would reduce the hardship of debt service, accelerate competition and produce more success, resulting in a better economic environment (growth). It also helps the monetary system to more easily bring economies out of recession or depression and keep them out.

3. *Increase the motivation of more individuals and businesses to invest in these systems as a way to further*

increase the availability of new money. In other words, increase the system's reserves.

4. *Education.* People should be made *aware of monetary power* in order to increase the debate for its betterment. Specific modes of improving monetary delivery systems need to be articulated. Discussions should not be limited to a better disclosure, regulation, supervision and operation of the current commercial and central banking systems and monetary policies. **We need to start the debate among the leaders and economists throughout the world.**

5. *Commercial banks and government bonds.* There should be less emphasis on government bonds and commercial banks for the delivery of new money to the economic environment. **The banks should still be the major issuers of new money but the amounts created should be reduced gradually as we implement new systems of delivery.**

6. *Excess inflation.* Do away with the idea that we should be trying to "eliminate inflation." Instead, economic debate should focus on eliminating "excess inflation."

7. *Growth.* It is time to question the definition of growth and its statistical measurements. It doesn't have to be measured to the nth degree or be excessively inflationary. Human economic hardship does not necessarily have to be induced to correct or improve the economic environment.

8. *Recirculation.* Recirculation of income overcoming one of the major flaws of capitalism is an absolute

necessity to have an adequate number of consumers in order to have a thriving economy.

9. *Effective monetary expansion.* Have an efficient, quality, growth-oriented monetary policy and system to increase commerce and velocity of circulation.

10. *Restructure* the economics of Federal governments.

OUR MONETARY SYSTEM

The major problem with capitalism is that governments do not increase the monetary supply in an efficient manner. This usually results in excessive debt or monetarization — ultimately promoting excessive inflation.

The current monetary system has experienced some major under diversification in its issuance of money. The end result has been stifled growth, employment and competition. The current monetary system discriminates against certain regions, individuals, industry, and only issues money through debt.

The world needs new capital to expand and employ. Private capital cannot do it alone. Governments have to reshape their monetary functions to meet the needs of a 21st century population.

I did not intend $E=mCf$ to be a book with all the facts, formal language, discussions of the current systems or new formulas. This is not a pure research-reference book with all the lengthy definitions, descriptions, explanations, histories, footnotes and credits. *My mission is to stimulate thought and encourage Federal leadership action to review the monetary structure of federal governments.*

It is time for the monetary side of government to come out of the closet. Let the people know what government is doing in terms of monetarization, off book items, guarantees, and the effects on the fiscal side, etc.

The public wants the government to provide services, lower taxes, balance budgets, solve problems and operate like a business. Therefore, the government should attempt to clearly display its operations, both fiscal and monetary. The government promotes commerce through fiscal side spending and lending on the monetary side. Yet, it receives a vast majority of its returns through taxation, and taxes are always being reduced (or at least, threatened to be reduced) by political forces.

≈≈≈≈

The common sense doctrine behind $E=mCf$ is an attempt to make the flaws of capitalism, fiscal systems and monetary policy and their relationship understandable to the masses and to effect revolutionary change.

In fact the entire discipline of economics has the wrong name. It should be named Humanomics. This title was coined by Eugene Loebel, an economist trained in socialism who converted to capitalism with his move to the U.S.

By changing the name from Economics to Humanomics, the major focus shifts from evaluating formulas, statistics and doctrines to improving the commercial success of more people and countries — the welfare of human beings.

We need to explore the solar system, the seas, cure diseases, stop urban blight, promote democracy and capitalism in the old soviet block and the third world nations. We are capable of accomplishing most of these tasks. *The only thing stopping us is macroeconomics.*

A properly empowered government with an intelligent mandate, both monetary and fiscal, can accomplish these objectives for the 21st century. *The current structure does not make common sense and any policy that combines both a constrictive fiscal and monetary policy can eventually, only be disastrous.*

Changing a major structure and operational system is very difficult to accomplish, especially in good times. Change has to be slow and gradual to reduce economic turbulence. I need everyone to join the effort to start the debate.

I urge economists from all over the planet to pick up the ball where the book leaves off, to develop original ways to operate our global monetary system. *I challenge this powerful community to diversify the monetary system.*

Loan this book out to others or encourage them to buy their own copies. Send letters to your leaders to read the book and begin the dialogue process. I welcome your help and your input. If you have any comments of suggestions, please email me at www.e-mcf@pash-benson.com. My web address is www.pash-benson.com. Or write me at the following address: Pash International Ltd Inc., PO Box 260874, Encino, California 91426-0874

And thank you for reading the book.

GLOSSARY OF TERMS

Aggregate Demand. The sum of all demand within an economy, making up national income and expenditure.

(Aggregate) **Supply**. The total of all goods and services produced in an economy, less exports, plus imports.

Annual deficit. An excess of expenditures over revenues (mostly taxes) received. This amount is borrowed and added to the national debt.

Anti-Trust. Legislation to control monopoly and restrictive practices that hinder competition.

Bankruptcy. A declaration by a court of law that an individual or company is insolvent, that is, cannot meet its debts on the due dates.

Bond. A form of loan (security) issued by central or local governments, companies, banks or other institutions. Bonds are usually a form of long-term debt (security or loan).

Bretton Woods. An international conference was held at Bretton Woods, New Hampshire, U.S.A. in July 1944 to discuss alternative proposals relating to post-war international payment problems put forward by U.S., Canadian and U.K. governments.

E=mC^f

Budget. An estimate of income and expenditures for a future period as opposed to actual receipts and expenditures.

Capacity. The maximum amount of goods and services that could be produced by a whole economy.

Capital gains. A realized increase in the value of a capital asset, as when a share or stock or real estate is sold for more than the price at which it was purchased.

Capital market. The market for longer term loanable funds as distinct from the short term funds. The capital market is an international one and is not one institution in any one country.

Capitalism. A social economic system in which individuals are free to own the means of production and maximize profits and in which resource allocation is determined by the price system.

Central bank. The instrument of the government's function to control the credit system and the power to create new money. A bankers' bank and lender of last resort. Federal Reserve is the central bank of the United States.

Commercial banks. Privately owned banks but regulated by government. Their major function is receiving deposits (savings accounts) and making loans to individuals, companies and other organizations.

Consumer Price Index (CPI). An index of prices of a specified basket of goods and services purchased by consumers to measure the rate of inflation or the cost of living.

Debt. A sum of money or other property owed by one person or organization to another. Debt requires debt servicing which consists of paying interest on the owed amount.

Deflation. A sustained reduction in the general levels of prices. Deflation is often, through not inevitably, accompanied by declines in output and employment.

Depression. An imprecise term given to a severe and prolonged economic downturn more severe than recession with a sustained high level of unemployment.

Developing country. A country that has not yet reached the stage of economic development characterized by the growth of industrialization, nor the level of national income sufficient to yield the domestic savings required to finance the investment necessary for further growth.

Economic growth. The increase in a country's per capita national income. There are problems in the measurement of national income; as many activities may not take place in a market where statistics are collected.

Economics. The study of production, distribution and consumption of wealth in human society. There never has been a definition that is acceptable to all.

Equity-ownership. The value of an asset after all outside debt (liabilities) have been satisfied, such as equity in your home. Stock in the stock market is considered equity.

$E=mC^f$

Exchange rate. The price (rate) at which one currency is exchanged for another currency.

Federal Reserve System. The central banking system of the United States, established by the Federal Reserve Act of 1913 and modified by the Banking Act 1935.

Fiscal power or policy. The ability of any government to collect taxes and spend whatever collections the policy determines can be taxed and spent.

Gross Domestic Product (GDP). A measure of the total flow of goods and services produced by the economy over a specific period of time. It is obtained by valuing outputs of goods and services at market prices and their aggregating.

Gross National Product (GNP). Gross domestic product plus the income to domestic residents arising from investment abroad, less income earned in the domestic market occurring to foreigners abroad.

Inflation. Persistent increases in the general level of prices.

Infrastructure. Roads, airports, sewage and water systems, railways, the telephone and other public utilities.

Interest rate. The proportion of a sum of money that is paid over a specified period of time in payment for its loan. It is the price a borrower has to pay to use cash which he does not own and the return a lender enjoys for deferring his consumption or parting with liquidity.

International Monetary Fund (IMF). It was set up by the UN Monetary and Financial Conference at Bretton Woods in 1944. The Fund was established to encourage international cooperation in the monetary field and the removal of foreign exchange restrictions, to stabilize exchange rates and to facilitate a multilateral payment system between countries.

Investment bank or Merchant Bank. A financial intermediary (old money) which purchases new issues and places them in smaller parcels among investors. Although called a bank, they are not the same as commercial banks who have new money creation ability.

Keynes economics. The branch of macroeconomic theory and doctrines that tends to support the following: [a] Aggregate demand plays a decreased role in determining the level of real output. [b] Economics can settle at positions with high unemployment and exhibit no natural tenancy for unemployment to fall. [c] Governments, primarily through fiscal policy, can influence aggregate demand to cut unemployment.

Keynes, John Maynard (1883 - 1946). English economist whose major work was the General Theory of Employment, Interest and Money.

Laissez-Faire. The principle of the non-intervention of government in economic affairs which is supported by classical economists who adopted the theme from Adam Smith in *Wealth of Nations*.

Loan. The borrowing of a sum of money by one person, company, government or other organization from another. Loans are debt and may be secured or unsecured, bearing interest or interest free, long-term or short term, redeemable or unredeemable.

Macroeconomics. The study of whole economic systems aggregating over the functioning of individual economic units. Macroeconomics is the study of national economies and the determination of national income.

Monetarism. The branch or theory of macroeconomics which holds that increases in the money supply are a necessary and sufficient condition for inflation and have a substantial effect in aggregate demand. Another tenet is that any change in aggregate demand the government succeeds in bringing about will manifest itself in the long run in higher prices and not higher output.

Monetary policy. A national government's policy with respect to the quantity of money in the economy.

Money supply. The stock of liquid assets in an economy which can freely be exchanged for goods or services. Money supply is a phrase that can describe anything from notes, bills, coin, cash, bank deposits, checks, money markets.

Monopoly. A market in which there is only one supplier.

National debt. The total outstanding borrowing of a central government (country).

Natural resources. Commodities or assets with some economic value which do not exist as a result of any effort of mankind, such as gold, silver, oil.

Open market operations. The purchase or sale of government bonds by the central bank to influence the supply of money, and so influence rates and the value of credit.

Recession. An imprecise term given to a sharp slow down in the rate of economic growth or a modest decline in economic activity.

Recirculation. Recirculation is a synonym of redistribution which means money is taken from the wealthiest and given to the less wealthy by taxation, usually increasing commerce if not too excessive.

Regulation. The supervision and control of the economic activities of private enterprise by government in the interest of economic efficiency, fairness, health and safety.

Socialism. A social and economic system in which the means of production are collectively owned (government) and equality is given a high priority.

Supply side economics. Concerns with the factors affecting the supply of goods and services in the economy.

Surplus. The amount of taxes and other revenue collected by governments over the amount of expenditures.

Usury. The act or practice of lending money at a rate of interest that is too high or against the law.

Velocity of circulation. The speed with which the money in an economy circulates or the number of times it is used for consumption of goods and services generating commerce, profits and taxes.

World Bank. The World Bank was set up by the Bretton Woods agreement of 1944. Its purpose was to encourage capital investment for the reconstruction and development of the member countries, either by channeling the necessary private funds or by making loans from its own resources.

MARK PASH, CFP, is a Certified Financial Planner with a bachelor's degree and a master's degree in business administration from UCLA and USC, respectively. Over the past 25 years Mark has been very active in the financial industry helping clients with their budgets, investments, loans, income taxes, social security, medical coverage and scores of other personal financial issues. Additionally, Mark has founded a number of financial organizations and has served as an officer of various industry corporations and associations. His unique background brings a grounded understanding of the practical and theoretical. Mark has long been involved in politics and was recently a Congressional candidate in Southern California. Mark has been married over 30 years to his wife Ruth and has two grown daughters, Andrea and Kimberly.

Mark Pash has written a number of articles on the subject of economic viability. *E=mCf the Theory of Economic Relativity*, is his first book.